Venturing
in Italy

Travels in Puglia,
Land between Two Seas

Venturing *in* Italy

Travels in Puglia, Land between Two Seas

Edited by Barbara J. Euser & Connie Burke

TRAVELERS' TALES
an imprint of Solas House
PALO ALTO

Travelers' Tales and *Travelers' Tales Guides* are trademarks of Travelers' Tales, an imprint of Solas House, 853 Alma Street, Palo Alto, California 94301.

For permission to print essays in this volume, grateful acknowledgement is made to the holders of copyright named on pages 220-231.

For more information on visiting Puglia, Italy, contact Regione Puglia at www.regione.puglia.it or the Italian Government Tourist Board at www.italiantourism.com.

Front and back cover photographs copyright by Connie Burke:
Front cover: *Trulli in Alberobello*; Back cover top: *Santa Cesarea waterfront*
Back cover bottom: *Baroque houses, Lecce*
Back cover photograph copyright by Barbara Euser: Top: *Single trullo in field*
All photosketches copyright by Connie Burke, with the exception of *Italian Mamma* and *Butcher shop, Alberobello* copyright by Laurie McAndish King

Cover and interior design by Sabine Reifig, Menta Design, Münster, Germany, www.mentadesign.de, using fonts Sloop (for initial letters), Trajan and Goudy.

CATALOGING DATA
Venturing in Italy: Travels in Puglia, Land between Two Seas/edited by Barbara J. Euser and Connie Burke.

    ISBN-10: 1-932361-64-2
    ISBN-13: 978-1932361-64-3

1. Italy—Description and travel. 2. Italy—Social life and customs.
3. Puglia—Description and travel. 4. Puglia—Social life and customs. I. Title.
II. Euser, Barbara J. III. Burke, Connie.

First Edition
Printed in the United States of America
10 9 8 7 6 5 4 3 2 1

To my daughters
Helane Isabella Euser Crowell
Jeanette Piper Euser Crowell

To my son
David Burke

CONTENTS

Contents

PREFACE

enturing in Italy: Travels in Puglia, Land between Two Seas is the product of a writers' workshop held in June 2008 in Puglia, Italy. For ten days, a group of nineteen writers, including instructors Linda Watanabe McFerrin and Joanna Biggar, Connie Burke and myself, criss-crossed the narrow peninsula, the heel of the boot of Italy that is Puglia.

Based in Alberobello, we lodged in *trulli*, the architecturally unique stone houses of the Valley of Itria. We visited the baroque city of Lecce, the archeological site of Egnazia, with its Messapii, Greek and Roman ruins, and Castello Svevo in the white city of Oria. We toured the austere octagonal Castel del Monte, and crossed the border into the neighboring province of Basilicata to tour the *sassi* (cave houses) of Matera. We relaxed at a day spa in Santa Cesarea, reveling in mud baths and massages. Famed singer and songwriter Al Bano Carrisi welcomed us to his estate and personally guided us through his *cantina*, home and record- ing studio. We toured wineries and ate at *masserie*. Every day, we enjoyed local culinary specialties at the fine restaurants scattered throughout Puglia and savored wines produced from native varieties of grapes.

These experiences inspired each writer to create pieces

reflecting the aspects of Puglia that he or she found most moving. Carol Kelly discovered unexpected musical ties to her native Jamaica. Chrysa Tsakopoulos and Roger Webster experienced mystical connections with the relics of their personal Orthodox saints. Denise Altobello found cultural parallels with her native New Orleans. Tom Harrell and I were intrigued by the ancient Messapian and Greek civilizations of Puglia. Doreen Wood deeply empathized with the *sassi* dwellers of Matera. Connie Burke indulged in—and wrote about—her favorite game, golf. Every writer was fascinated and charmed by the Puglian country-side, from its rolling hills and open valleys to its seaside cliffs and sandy beaches.

I hope you enjoy accompanying the writers as they make their own personal discoveries of the sights and sounds of Puglia. May this book inspire you to travel to Puglia to make personal discoveries of your own.

—Barbara J. Euser

Acknowledgments

We would like to express our deep appreciation to Regione Puglia for inviting us to experience the fascinating culture, landscape and history of the province. From our first meeting with Mr. Alfredo Deliguori in Bari to the expressions of support we received from Directors Dr. Annamaria Maiellaro and Dr. Marina Cancellara, we received the warmest possible welcome. Ms. Lucrezia Mastrolonardo of Cotup, Puglia's consortium of tourist operators, assisted us with our itinerary and Ms. Marilù Vaccarini served as our informative, unfailingly cheerful guide.

We savored memorable meals at La Cantina, Trulli D'Oro, Casa Nova and Don Carmelo's Ristorante Pizzeria in Alberobello; La Sommita Relais in Ostuni; Ristorante L'Ancora in Monopoli; Hotel Ristorante Orsa Maggiore in Castro Marina; Ristorante Alla Corte di Hyria in Oria; Tenute Pedale Masseria, near Andria; Tenute Al Bano Carrisi, near Brindisi; Masseria Cantone, near Ostuni; Osteria dagli Angeli, Lecce; Riva dei Tessali Golf Club and Resort, near Taranto.

We would also like to thank the Gruppo Folkloristico "Città dei Trulli," directed by Mr. Nino Agostino Costumi, for the charming demonstration of folk dancing given for us by its children's ensemble; Professor Pino Alvo who guided us enthusiastically through the historical monuments of Oria; and Ms. Maria Teresa Cofano who provided us with our first introduction to her home province.

We would like to personally thank Ms. Antonella Guido and Mr. Dino Barnaba of Trullidea Resort in Alberobello for their congeniality and the assistance they provided to all the writers during our stay in their collection of beautifully restored, authentic trulli.

We would like to thank all the friendly, open people of Puglia who graciously received us in their rich and captivating region.

—Barbara J. Euser

ILLUSTRATIONS

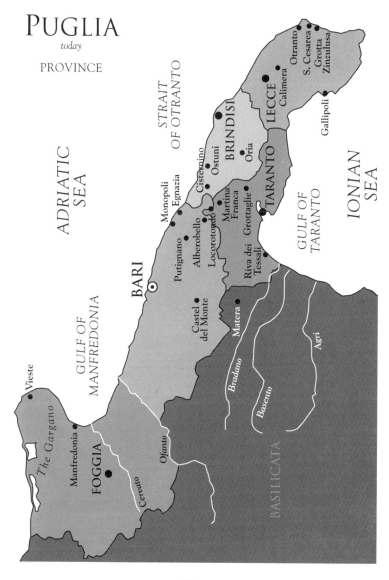

PUGLIA
today

PROVINCE

STRAIT OF OTRANTO

ADRIATIC SEA

IONIAN SEA

Otranto
S. Cesarea
Grotta
Zinzulusa

LECCE

Calimera

BRINDISI

Gallipoli

Ostuni
Cisternino
Oria

TARANTO

Monopoli
Egnazia

Martina
Franca
Grottaglie

GULF OF TARANTO

Putignano
Alberobello
Locorotondo

Riva dei
Tessali

BARI

Castel
del Monte

Matera

GULF OF MANFREDONIA

Bradano

Basento

Agri

Vieste

The Gargano

Manfredonia

FOGGIA

Ofanto

Cervaro

BASILICATA

SEEING GREEN IN GARGANO

JOANNA BIGGAR

*F*rom a distance, the waters off the seaside town of Vieste shimmer in a thousand shades of Mediterranean blue. But dive into those waters off any of Vieste's long, sandy beaches, look back at the whitewashed town atop limestone cliffs embraced by long arms of forested land, and suddenly the sea appears green. Perhaps that trick of the eye is the best symbol for the Gargano, called the spur of the Italian boot, a promontory that cuts jaggedly into the Adriatic in Puglia's northeast corner, for the entire region comprises a national park.

When I was the swimmer lazily drifting in that water contemplating the unspoiled land and seascape, I began to wonder how green, in the environmental sense, the Gargano is, and how different it really is from the rest of Puglia and southern Italy. Trying to unravel these questions, as is often the case in Italy, I found the answers complex. Yes, the south suffers from the despoilment of "progress," even as there are measures in place to save its inherent beauty. And, yes, surely the Gargano, with it deep forests, high cliffs and clean beaches reigns as the Green Queen of Puglia.

The south in general is recognized as one of the most unspoiled parts of Italy, with miles of undeveloped coastline, scattered quaint towns and villages, the vast wheat fields and vineyards of Puglia, and an estimated fifty million olive trees, some claimed to be one thousand years old. Yet it has also always been prone to natural disasters: earthquakes, drought, landslides, volcanoes. And, since its occupation by the Romans, the south has been no stranger to environmental degradation as the price of progress. Indeed it was the Romans who deforested most of Puglia to turn its rich flat lands and rolling hills into wheat fields, making it Italy's breadbasket, which it has been ever since. But by denuding the land, they also created malarial marshes that brought the ravages of a devastating disease to a people who suffered from it for over two thousand years. Yet the Gargano, isolated and rugged, escaped the Roman scythes and its forests remain intact.

In modern times, energy needs and industrialization have wreaked their own havoc, particularly in larger cities. For example, Foggia, the capital of the province of Foggia which encompasses the Gargano, is Puglia's most industrialized city, and the least attuned to tourism while Bari, the administrative capital for all of Puglia, hides its charming ancient center within unattractive rings of factories and commercial zones. And the port city of Brindisi, which harbors the Enel power station, is ranked by the World Wildlife Fund as Europe's ninth largest producer of carbon dioxide. In fact, Puglia houses the three top carbon dioxide sites in all of Italy. Yet the Gargano, with no big or industrialized cities, apart from Manfredonia on its flat, southern coast, and a few moderate-sized towns tucked into its mountains or rocky coastline, seems far removed from these concerns.

Though environmental problems exist in the south, so do remedies. There are studies of dune restoration and air pollution, plans for reducing electricity production in Brindisi by 25 percent over ten years to be in compliance with the Kyoto Protocol, and wind farms near Foggia, to name a few. In addition to governmental efforts, the European Union has committed to a program for sustainable growth in Puglia for 2007-2013 that is one of the largest in Italy.

Of course the Gargano, where the environmental concerns focus particularly on the negative effect of too much tourism, will also benefit from such plans for preservation and sustainability. But in many ways the Gargano is another country, both in topography and in conservation.

If you take the road from Manfredonia along the coast to Vieste, as I did, you will have left behind the dry, thirsty scrub and flat plains to scenes familiar to any Californian: desert-like hill country giving way to pine-covered limestone hills showing their age in the striated, crumbling layers of sediment left by millions of years of tectonic uplift. Then, as you climb into those hills, you enter a realm of lush beauty, villas overflowing with bougainvillea, palm trees, bountiful pink and white oleander, geraniums and leggy gold and yellow lantana. Soon the hills have become cliffs and then the cliffs give way to an astonishing view of the whitewashed buildings of Vieste and the sea, where if you are lucky, as I was, you may soon swim. This might be a favorite spot elsewhere in Italy, along the Riviera perhaps, or the Amalfi coast, but for those long green arms of forest.

It is after all the forest that makes the Gargano different. The south's usual olive and almond groves mix with pines that, as you climb into the mountains, become thick with beech, maple, chestnuts, fir and ancient oaks, some more than two thousand years old, and animals more typical of Central Europe than Italy. This is because the peninsula was once part of modern Croatia, across the Adriatic, then was separated from the land when two tectonic plates pulled apart to form the sea. For untold time it was an island until, during the Ice Age, silt filled in and connected it to what is now Italy.

So to truly experience the Gargano, you must venture into its deepest forest, the Foresta Umbra, the Forest of the Shadows, one of the few remaining nearly wild places in Italy. Its fifteen thousand hectares of relict woods are thick with birds, wildlife and a dazzling array of flora, much of it exotic. Over two thousand species of plants, shrubs and flowers, including rare orchids, mountain anemones and peonies are found in the shadows of the forest, giving rise to its unofficial title as "a botanical museum of the Italian peninsula." Moreover, 138 fauna species are designated "transadriatic," because they actually descended from creatures in the Balkans from the period before the Gargano separated from the Central European mainland.

Small winding roads lead through the forest which is laced with well-marked hiking trails and lined with shaded picnic tables. In high summer, when temperatures along the coast can soar to over 100° F, an escape to the cool of the forest provides welcome relief. At its center is the Corpo Forestale, or park headquarters, a building harboring a small museum, information and maps. It is the best place to get an overview of what lies within the shadowy woods. There, in glass cases and on the walls are plant specimens, photographs and stuffed animals. Deer, elk, snakes, hedgehogs, martens, bobcats and wolverines occupy the forest floor, while birds as varied as falcons, hawks, small game birds and doves dominate its skies.

Among the displays at the headquarters is a map showing the region as part of the holdings of the once-powerful Grimaldi family, who now rule the small country of Monaco. Perhaps these aristocratic overlords helped keep the forest intact as a hunting preserve, but that is just my guess. In any event, the Foresta Umbra became an officially protected area in 1891, putting the Gargano in the vanguard of environmental protection.

Then one hundred years later, in order to stop encroaching

development, the promontory was declared the Parco Nationale del Gargano, making it the only national park in Puglia.

The Gargano seems likely to remain a pristine haven, as long as development is restricted and tourism controlled. In addition to its forests, the Gargano is also blessed with waterways of heart-stopping beauty. There are two saltwater lakes, Lago di Lesina and Lago di Varano on the northern side of the promontory, miles of dramatic coastline, and coves, beaches, caves and hundreds of magical grottos that are huge attractions to visitors. But in particular, the Isole Tremiti, an archipelago of three islands thirty-six miles offshore is a major draw. Within an hour's boat ride over glittering seas from the mainland, you can see towering limestone cliffs, pine forests, quaint medieval towns and the largest and loveliest of many grottos, Grotto del Bue Marino. No wonder over one hundred thousand tourists visit in July and August every year. And no wonder environmentalists worry.

But I have to confess that worry—about anything—was hard to come by in the Gargano. At least for me. With sun and a sense of space, lovely villages whitewashed or carved of limestone, flowers spilling over ancient walls, the scents of rich food cooking close by and the prospect of a flavorful local wine soon to be decanted, it was difficult to work up to worry. Perhaps that sense of well-being is a trick of the mind, like the changes in color are a trick of the eye. But I do recommend it. Try floating on your back off one of the Gargano's glorious beaches, look back at the embrace of the forest as it comes down to meet the shore and think of the wonders of the wild in the Foresta Umbra which crowns the rest. Then watch the shade of the water turn beneath you. Maybe you, too, will be seeing green.

At Home in a Masseria

ELEANOR SHANNON

The baby girl in the arms of her father is the only person smiling in the black and white family photo on the wall of my room in the Masseria Cimino. In the center front, two older women stand together in the waning light of the afternoon. They look like sisters. One wears flat, black shoes and a dark dress. Her left arm is held up at an awkward angle by a black sling. The other has a long white apron tied solidly around her thick middle in a way that accentuates her heavy breasts. She gazes down at the ground with a vacant stare.

I wonder about the women in this photograph. If they could see the Masseria Cimino today, would they believe that sophisticated visitors from around the world come here to experience the authenticity and simplicity of Puglian food, wine and family traditions?

This *masseria* (fortified farm), like hundreds of others, was originally part of a feudal system used for over five hundred years by Spaniards and Bourbons to dominate Puglia and protect the Adriatic Coast from Saracen pirates. Even long after the oppressors left, life on these farms was hard, as Puglia lagged behind the rest of Italy in its development.

In the last ten or fifteen years, however, the *masserie* have been the backbone of a rapid rise in tourism in Puglia. Visitors can choose from a complete range of *masserie*: from the most basic *agriturismo*-style bed and breakfast on a family farm all the way up to places like the Masseria San Domenico, which was built as a sixteenth century watchtower and is, now, a five-star fifty-room hotel. When I first arrived in Puglia, the unabashed luxury of the San Domenico seduced me into staying for three days of decadent relaxation. There was a freeform saltwater pool, a private beach, a golf course and a chic "thalasso therapy" spa.

As I was leaving, Marisa Melpignano, the founder and owner, had said, "Listen, you really have to go over and see the Masseria Cimino. My sister runs it as a guest house on the edge of the San Domenico golf course."

"*Hmmm . . .*" I thought, "*Maybe I will stop by.*" Fifteen minutes later, I entered the reception area. There was a taller than average woman with shoulder length brown hair at the desk. I approached her, introduced myself, explained that Marisa had sent me, and asked if I could speak with Signora Annamaria Lisi. The woman's tanned face broke into a warm smile and her soft eyes laughed at me. "I am Annamaria Lisi!" she had replied, "I always work at the reception desk on weekends to give my desk staff a break."

I looked around at the whitewashed walls of this stone *masseria*. It was small and intimate compared to the San Domenico. The furnishings, all white or light grey, gave a feeling of freshness and simplicity. Well-used iron farm tools and cactus pads hung in attractive patterns on the walls. Their starkness gave the impression of contemporary art, but also served as a reminder of how hard it had once been to eke a living out of the dry, sun-baked Puglian soil.

I remembered what the *padrone* of the Casa Nova restaurant in Alberobello, Ignazio Spinetti, had told me a few days earlier when he gave me his grandmother's recipe for a Puglian staple called *le fave 'ngrapiate* (a single dish of pureed fava beans, potatoes, olive oil, leftover bread, vegetables and onion that could be served as a "one-plate" meal).

"Food was scarce, Signora. We could only eat meat once or twice a year. Our mothers and grandmothers had to find ways to fill our empty stomachs with only the simplest ingredients. The most precious moments of the day were when we gathered to eat."

Although food is anything but scarce at the Masseria Cimino now, mealtimes are special. That first afternoon, I asked Annamaria if the *masseria* served lunch. She responded, "It's not a proper lunch, but Rosa can bring you something light."

Eating the simple bowl of *orecchiette* there on the terrace of the *masseria* produced a feeling of intense connection with the past while living in the beauty and pleasure of the moment. I felt a kind of magic and lightness as I drank in not only the wine, but the scene: sun, sea, earth and sky.

The thick, twisted roots of the olive trees in front of me reminded me of how deeply Puglia is grounded in its tradition and history. From the terrace, I could see the ancient walls of the Greek and Roman city of Egnazia running along the edge of the olive grove just to my left. Directly in front of me was the road that the Emperor Trajan had built as an extension of the Appian Way from Rome to Brindisi. And, Annamaria had just told me that the *masseria* sits atop a *necropoli* (underground burial sites) of the Messapian people, who lived at Egnazia even earlier in the fifth century BCE.

Every *masseria* in Puglia, whether simple or deluxe, enthusiastically serves sumptuous meals featuring Puglian specialties with the stated objective of making visitors feel "at home." The Masseria Tenuta Pedale represents *agriturismo* at its finest. Built in 1600 on the peaceful plains below Castel del Monte near the Adriatic Sea, this fortified *masseria* is nestled in a grove of oak, olive and fruit trees interspersed with endless rows of grapevines. Our writers' group enjoyed a lengthy organic lunch of fresh-picked tomatoes, eggplant parmigiana and zucchini followed by estate-made lamb and pork sausages. The wine and olive oil, like everything on the menu, is produced on the farm. Fresh cherries are picked while you eat and served for dessert.

In the area between Bari and Brindisi, there are many *masserie* in addition to the San Domenico and the Cimino. For example, the Masseria Don Sante and the Masseria Alchimia are bed and breakfast *agriturismi*. The Masseria Il Frantoio near Ostuni is an organic farm producing olive oil with eight guest rooms and a riding stable so that guests can bring their own horses! The Masseria Torre Coccaro and the Masseria Torre Maizza, two five-star hotels near Savelletri on the sea, offer an Aveda spa, a cooking school, a private beach, pools and horseback riding.

At the end of our Puglian sojourn, we had dinner at the Masseria Cantone near Cisternino. We arrived by a narrow winding road through rolling hills of olive trees, entered through a *cancello* (iron gate) and followed a candlelit path through a lush garden to the front door. There were five apartments with kitchenettes for overnight guests, a swimming pool and bicycles available for touring the area. The *masseria's* dining room had a high ceiling with square windows hovering well above our heads, once a necessary part of defending food stores, animals and the family from invaders. Greeted by tall thin glasses of chilled white wine produced by the *masseria*, we feasted until we could eat and drink no more.

On the morning of the summer solstice, my next to last day at the Masseria Cimino, I woke up at 5:30. The sun was coming up above the long, flat line of blue sea, just visible from my bed. I pulled on my swimsuit, threw on a t-shirt, grabbed a towel and walked five minutes across the *masseria's* olive grove toward the sea.

I knew from previous explorations that the dirt path on the other side of the road led to a small sandy beach between the rocky outcroppings of the coastline. The waves, wind and current were blowing onshore. I dove in and floated on my back. I could feel the warmth of the sun on my face as the cool, salty water flowed over me. "*Coccolle del mare* (Caresses of the sea)," I thought to myself. The Messapians, Greeks and Romans probably swam here and the landscape has changed very little since then. Walking back to the *masseria*, the wind and sun dried my back and shoulders.

In my rustic but elegant room, I looked at the faces of the family photo once again. This time, I felt connected, almost a part of their family. I wished I could talk with them. It seemed that the women would be proud of Marisa and Annamaria: two sisters, who had left Puglia to spend thirty years in Rome, but had come home to their *masserie* giving each a certain style and personality. I knew that it would be hard to leave the next day. I was at home in the *masseria*.

THE HEEL OF THE BOOT

CONNIE GUTOWSKY

I spend an hour sitting in the town square in Lecce early one evening in June. A white-haired man pushes a younger one in a wheelchair. People walk, some with canes, some wearing canvas flats, sandals, or boots, coming and going across the cobblestones. You can buy a stamp here at the *tobaccaio* (tobacco store), a sparkling water at the BAR, a pair of hand-made earrings from a street vendor. The music of Italian conversation mingles as swallows swoop and chirp amongst the old buildings. More bicycles are visible than cell phones. Olive and citrus trees thrive in their large planter boxes, greening the square. A small police car drives by with windows down. Teenagers call to one another. Girls meet with a kiss to each cheek, handbags draping off shoulders. There are plenty of places to sit and rest weary feet, to sip or smoke. Small groups of men in

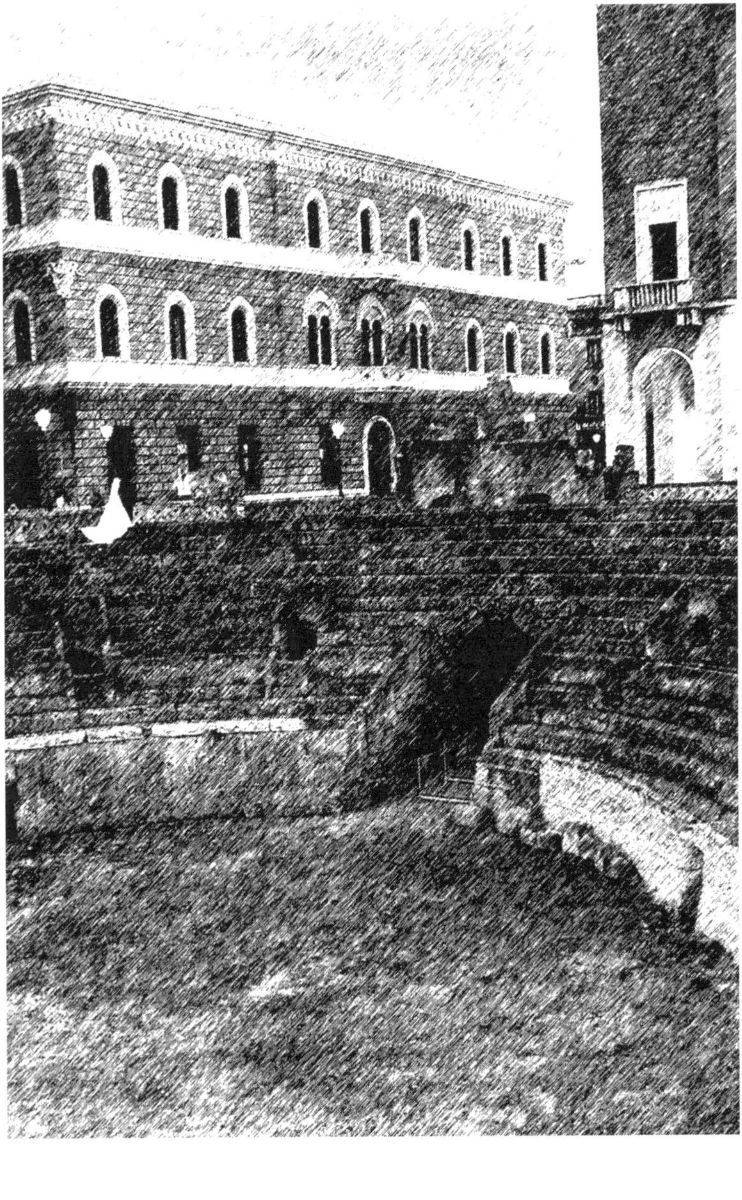

short sleeves sit and talk with gesture and nod, intent in discussion. Couples of all ages walk arm in arm. Little girls skip along, smiling, one hand held by their *mamma*, one by their *nonna*. As church bells chime eight, a bride and groom walk at the edge of the square with attendants carrying bouquets and small presents, then disappear around the corner, a Roman amphitheater just steps away.

First thing in the morning, Nicola, our broad-shouldered tour-bus driver whose dark eyes miss nothing, quips as we drive from Alberobello, a UNESCO world heritage site, "all the lawyers in Milan have bought a summer home here." For hundreds of centuries Puglia was bedeviled with serial invasions by foreigners who were drawn to its mild climate and strategic geographical position: gateway to Europe, to Greece and to the Orient. Now there is a new kind of invader, the tourist, and I am one.

The British actress Helen Mirren has acquired a castle in Tiggiano in southern Puglia. The demand for restored *masserie* (traditional fortified stone farmhouses) is outstripping supply. These single storey homes built around a courtyard are Romanesque in style. Living rooms, formerly workers' rooms, have vaulted stone ceilings and handmade fireplaces. Bedrooms with baths were once stables. You can hear the sound of fountains trickling outside beside lemon trees. The renovations, thought to be a good investment, are selling for five hundred thousand to one million euro and more. It has become fashionable for northerners to spend their holidays here. Budget European airlines fly into Bari and Brindisi providing easy access to Puglia.

The landscape is like a magnificent fertile garden. Puglia is called "the California of Italy" producing spring vegetables for all of Italy and again in fall, reliably growing grapes for wine, and durum wheat for flour. Almond, pomegranate, orange, lime and lemon trees blossom in spring and produce abundant yields. Puglia's unusual architecture, gentle lifestyle and current prosperity belie the legacy of deprivation. She is now the wealthiest region in southern Italy.

For centuries farming was dominated by *latifondi* (large extensively cultivated estates of absentee landlords) and managed by middlemen who paid subsistence wages to an impoverished peasantry. Wheat was inter-cropped on the same fields with grapevines and olive trees in many areas. A bad year for one of these three major crops, no matter where, was typically accompanied by a bad year for another. This was due to the rainfall pattern and scarce groundwater. A particularly hot dry summer increased the chance of crop failure. The risky environment meant crop output uncertainty. Farmers suffered substantial income instability. Access to *cassi rurali* (rural credit cooperatives) was unavailable or very limited. Poor farmers had inadequate financial facilities, an absence of techniques for watering crops, and a harsh climate, all of which contributed to Puglia's reputation for backwardness.

Though conquests, subjugation and poverty characterize Puglia's history, it prospers now. Today, instructional tours are being organized by the French, who are interested in Napoleonic history, Romanesque architecture, and wines; by the Russians who have an interest in Saint Nicholas, buried in Bari; by the Germans who are interested in the influence of King Frederick II; and by Americans who often come to Puglia while on a cruise and want to return. The trend is not to stay in a large hotel in a city, but in a smaller place where spa treatments are being made available, or in a *masseria* where meals are cooked and served family-style.

On my last day in Puglia I think about how the resilient Pugliese have so generously shared their way of life and their unique history. If "the fountains alone justify a trip to Rome," as Shelly proclaimed, the feel of old Italia justifies a visit to Puglia, the heel of the boot.

Waist-ing Away in Puglia

Laurie McAndish King

To paraphrase a well-known aphorism, *a journey of one thousand excesses begins with a single bite*. And—one single bite after another—I happily ate my way through Puglia, in southern Italy. Anticipating the visit was a gastronomic adventure in itself. Puglia has a long coastline, an agricultural heritage and a tradition of frugality. It is known for healthful and unpretentious cuisine, influenced by centuries of interactions, whether by trade or invasion, with Greeks, Byzantines, Arabs, French and Spaniards.

My heart was set on tasting the local specialties, particularly the superb seafood, *burrata* (a rich, fresh mozzarella) and *orecchiette* pasta. But my heart—and my waistline—expanded to embrace lowly vegetables, ripe fruit and humble bread as gourmet highlights. In Puglia, I discovered, fine food and folkways combine to make an irresistible repast.

Our culinary experiences, which I quickly came to regard as orgies of the very best kind, typically began between one and two o'clock in the afternoon and lasted until three-thirty or four, once even five o'clock. As in many other countries, the long meal here is timed to coincide with the hot afternoon sun, which precludes heavy labor both indoors and out. But no matter what one's vocation, a meal in a hurry is an unthinkable insult in Italy, where sharing food is one of life's simple—and essential—pleasures. And the fact that the event was stretched out over such a long period of time somehow made my holiday gluttony seem almost acceptable.

We ate at least five courses at each meal, beginning with antipasti. These were typically five or six small, very flavorful dishes, such as mozzarella tied into a small knot (*nodino*) or fresh seafood. Often there would be julienned beets or carrots dressed with olive oil and vinegar. Ristorante Orsa Maggiore's antipasti included zucchini flowers fried in a light, tempura-like batter; and *pittule*, a fried croquette-like dish made with a batter of flour, potato and yeast surrounding a bit of blanched cauliflower. I never managed to choose among the antipasti. In fact, I felt compelled to try every one—in the name of culinary research—and a small bite never seemed to be quite enough. The antipasti were offered in such quantity and variety that I was inevitably satisfied after sampling them, but the main meal was yet to come.

After the antipasti we were presented with a "first course" of pasta and a "second course" of meat, the portions of which were inevitably generous and understandably quite filling. These were followed by a palate-cleansing raw vegetable course at which slices of carrot, cucumber or *finocchio* (fennel bulb) might be served. At the restaurant Trullo d'Oro we cleared our palates with raw slices of a pale green, slightly sweet vegetable called *carocello*, specific to this region, which reminded me of a honeydew melon and others of a cucumber. Next came the fresh fruit course featuring sweet watermelon slices; perfect, firm-but-juicy Bing cherries; small, tart apricots and sweet plums during our June visit. We finished with cookies or a cake course and then a serving, if one dared, of strong *limoncello* liqueur. An espresso was available to top it off.

The meals were so huge and so delicious that I began to eat myself sick on a daily basis. And I began making promises to God: every day, I swore that if I could only finish this one last meal—sampling just a bite or two of everything that was offered—and then make it through the afternoon, I would never again overindulge. Every afternoon I pictured myself virtuously pushing away from the table at the *next* meal, maintaining my figure and my health. And every evening I sinned again, salivating the instant I saw the menu.

Mussels were among the most difficult to resist. Don Carmelo Ristorante Pizzeria served them in the peasant style—that is, combined with other ingredients into a one-dish meal, characteristic of this part of Italy because it was faster for working families both to prepare and to consume. Preparing a mussel *tiella* (casserole) is quick and simple: slices of zucchini and onion are layered together in a baking pan. Chunks of peeled potatoes are added and steamed, opened mussels in their shells are arranged on top, then layered with rinsed rice and sliced tomatoes. Finish with pecorino cheese and breadcrumbs and bake in a hot oven for half an hour.

One taste and I became a mussel maniac. When cooked, the smooth, flesh-like morsels tightened and huddled—warm and peach-colored, sweet and tender—at the edge of their rough blue-black shells. They hunkered there, clinging, small and succulent, as if anticipating the approach of my hungry tongue and teeth. The mussels' slippery folds released trickles of the dish's rich juices, inviting exploration (and simultaneously providing plenty of selenium, vitamin B12, zinc and folate). I savored them at every opportunity.

Another local staple is *purea di fave* (broadbean puree). Many broadbean recipes call for the addition of cooked potatoes or a little milk for smoothness and to extend the dish. The heavy, pale puree is traditionally served with bread and a counterbalancing *cicorie*—wild chicory, salted and boiled, then cooked up with olive oil to a deep, bitter green. In the one-dish version, the chicory and fried cubes of dry bread called *cecamariti* ("husband-blinders") are stirred together with the bean puree.

The origin of the expression "husband-blinders" to describe food is not clear. The most likely explanation, in my opinion, is that leftovers are used to create a dish so tasty that it dazzles—or blinds—a husband into thinking his wife has slaved for hours in the kitchen. But there is also the possibility the expression was used to describe a dish so filling it will placate a hungry husband, or a meal so delicious it will drive a husband to overeat, and subsequently to fall asleep. My favorite explanation suggests that *cecamariti* have the power of "putting husbands to bed, leaving wives free to meet their lovers."

Husband-blinding may be the most picaresque of Puglia's culinary traditions, but it is certainly not the only one. Fortified farmhouses—called *masserie*—dating from the sixteenth and seventeenth centuries dot the landscape. Inside, the *masserie* resembled agricultural factories: wheat was separated, grapes and olives were crushed, and cheese was made. Today, converted *masserie* continue their tradition as an important part of Italy's agritourism industry, providing intimate venues for weddings, cooking classes, romantic vacations and wellness spas. They still use house-grown or locally produced fruits and vegetables and often make their own wine, cheese and olive oil.

At Masseria Tenuta Pedale the fresh fruits and vegetables were irresistible. Here I discovered a delicious way to prepare carrots: *sott'olio* (under oil), parboiled and served with capers and a sprinkle of salt. Zucchini and eggplant are also traditionally prepared *sott'olio*: first they are salted and weighted to draw out moisture, then they are julienned, simmered with a little vinegar and water, cooled and dressed with garlic, mint and a drizzle of extra virgin olive oil. Trullo d'Oro in Alberobello served beet-roots prepared in a similar fashion. I had expected balsamic vinegar or perhaps red wine vinegar, but in Puglia a simple white vinegar suffices.

At Trullo d'Oro I also enjoyed a perfect plate of *orecchiette* (little ears), another specialty of the region. These small pieces of pasta were traditionally made by local women, who pulled a bit of dough off a larger piece and used their forefingers to poke it into a "little ear," ideally shaped for catching and retaining sauces. My favorite way to eat *orecchiette* was with a sauce of hot fresh tomato chunks, a shaving of hard Pecorino cheese and fresh basil leaves. Something about this dish made me feel very naughty, as though I were actually chewing on the ears of little children, so I was tempted to hurry through it. But a perfectly al dente mouthful requires that one slow down and savor the flavors and textures.

La Cantina in Alberobello served one of the most irresistible culinary temptations: *burrata,* a local mozzarella that is simply, deliciously addictive. A large *burrata* is the size of an orange, a small one more like an egg. In fact, it reminds me of a soft-boiled egg, although round rather than oval in shape, with an outside layer the consistency of cooked egg white. Inside, a silky white melding of fresh mozzarella and cream bursts from its round white rind and spills forth like a soft-boiled yolk, oozing onto the plate, running together with the pool of golden olive oil that sits beneath the cheese. The taste is as creamy as one would expect, yet light enough that I could eat quite a lot—and I did.

Luckily for cheese lovers like myself, the companionably hearty Pugliese bread was served everywhere, its light, yeasty fragrance wafting from each restaurant table. Loaves have been made in the same way for centuries, and are deservedly world famous. Legend has it that the Roman poet Horace described them in 37 BCE as "by far the best bread to be had, so good that the wise traveler takes a supply of it for his onward journey."

Traditionally, Pugliese bread was baked into large loaves with an exceptionally crunchy crust for a long shelf life—easy to send off with a working husband who might be fishing or herding sheep for days at a time. Dense and pale straw-colored, its ingredients are hard wheat flour, water, salt and *biga*, a yeasted starter. Multiple long rise cycles and baking at gradually decreasing temperatures are the secrets to producing the chewy loaf; spritzing with water as it bakes produces the characteristic crust. Pugliese bread is even useful when stale; it is porous enough to absorb other ingredients and therefore ideal for making *crostini* and *bruschetta*, lightly toasted bread slices spread with olive oil, cheese, tomato, meat sauce or other savory toppings. And of course it is essential for the infamous *cecamariti*.

Good as Pugliese bread is, Il Gioiello (The Jewel) in Alberobello has improved it. Their version, dotted with crunchy almonds and liberally studded with chunks of dried fig—ripe, sweet and moist—served steaming hot, is the most delicious bread I have ever tasted. It was served with a sampling of fig jam, onion marmalade, and *marmellata di peperoncino e cioccolato*—a remarkable conserve of rich, dark chocolate spiced up with hot peppers. As I perused the menu, I made a mental note to follow Horace's advice and stock up on a few loaves for my onward journey.

And the figs! In Oria, Alla Corte di Hyria's figs with balsamic reduction were so succulent they inspired me to a *When Harry Met Sally*-like dining performance. Warm sweet fig halves slid into my mouth like oysters; their soft, furry skin a welcome surprise. Eyes closed, head tilted back, I settled into a moment of gustatory ecstasy, the fig's firm roundness heavy on my tongue, until the sweet-sharp tang of a sugared balsamic reduction filled my mouth and returned me to consciousness. Which was a good thing, because I would not have wanted to miss the rich, earthy flavors of *crostini con crema di tartufo*: rounds of crunchy toast topped with creamy truffle spread.

L'Ancora (The Anchor) in Monopoli served one of our finest meals, a two-and-a-half hour festival that began with a surprisingly tender little octopus. One bite followed another as we moved to what may well have been the most exquisite dish of our visit: lobster-drenched spaghetti. The silky sauce was deep adobe in color, thick and bisque-like, intensely flavored with lobster and peppered with small pieces of the sweet seafood. Ironically, this is the one dish I had tasted at home. Or perhaps it is not a coincidence at all that one of the finest recipes of the region should have been appropriated. In an attempt to recreate the meal in my own kitchen, I googled "recipe for spaghetti with lobster sauce" and got 156,000 results. If only I knew which one L'Ancora used.

But my final large meal in Alberobello was by far the most memorable. Bepe, a docent in the olive oil museum, invited my fellow travel writer Chrysa and me to his family's home in a multi-domed *trulli* in the countryside beyond Alberobello. Outside, olive and almond trees circled the house and huge, pink-blooming hydrangea brightened the front yard. Inside, a gay multicolored tablecloth peeked out from beneath more than a dozen dishes Bepe's mother had prepared for her family, the in-laws and cousins who lived next door, their grandfather and ourselves. I surreptitiously undid the button at my waistline and settled in for the feast.

The locally caught octopus was tender, light and delicious. Cold, thin slices of beef served with a smooth sauce of mayonnaise and tuna were equally appealing. A cool *insalata di riso* (rice salad) proved perfect for the hot day: pieces of tuna and sausage provided protein, and the light dressing of lemon juice and olive oil with capers added enough sharpness to balance the flavor. Bepe's family shared anchovies and omelets, salad, bread, olives, cucumber, pizza, cheeses and more. Then we moved outside for fruit, two cakes, gelato and *limoncello*. Not speaking Italian, I missed much of the conversation, but the hospitality was unmistakable. As my journey of one thousand excesses drew to a close, another maxim twisted in my imagination: *A waist is a terrible thing to mind.*

THE GALLO OF GROTTAGLIE

ETHEL F. MUSSEN

"*Fondato a 1624*" declares the legend over the entrance to the ceramics workshop in the old city of Grottaglie. "Fasano Nicola" is the name above the date, the ancestor of the seven brothers who produce and sell the *maioliche* or faience—tin-glazed earthenware—seen throughout Puglia. Grandfather Francesco introduced the saucy rooster to his early dishes so diners would have chicken on their plates every day of the year. It became a trademark of the workshop and the genre and a pattern popular with the public—a jaunty center bordered by blue-dotted rosettes and simple rim line.

Now his grandson, Francesco, the *padrone* of the factory demonstrates his skill at the decorator's bench for the visiting *giornalistas*. Deftly he strokes in the comb and tail feathers to the rotund body, then outlines the slim legs and feet, and lo, the *gallo* crows in the plate. The cock abounds here in the stacks of bowls and plates in his shop across the lane but is also seen in the many *ristorantes* of Puglia who buy his tableware. Its ubiquitous presence throughout the region piqued my curiosity about the number of factories and shops. I learn that each of the seven brothers and one sister has his/her own shop. Also, this *Quartiere Ceramiche* (Ceramic Quarter) boasts fifty retail shops in contrast to the dwindling numbers in other such centers. Since I collect earthenware in France and Italy, I am familiar with the edgy competition among neighboring potters in the changing market. Internecine jockeying among siblings adds battle to the art and the commerce. One brief visit does not provide enough time to probe the intimate heart of the community, and I must remain curious as to who creates, and who survives.

Just in this small corner three shops boast different Fasano given names and abut the factory carved out of the tufa hill. Twenty workers ply their craft here: forming, shaping, mixing, glazing, firing and decorating. Francesco reveals a total of thirty employees who make, sell or promote his wares in Italy, London and New York. Though Francesco Fasano's factory is the largest and perhaps the most popular, the ceramic wares of his competitors are equally impressive with their own historical and familial significance.

Inside Francesco's factory, he leads us to the potter's wheel. He points to the photograph of his twenty-five-year-old self, turning a vase. "That was twenty-two years ago," he boasts, stroking his still-dark hair.

Just below the picture, we watch stocky Cosimo as he pedals the same wheel to hollow out an emerging *pupa*, one of the trademark figures of Grottaglie. The skirt swells and is decorated with a comb-like instrument to make a pattern, then the waistline is delineated, the bosom shaped. The graceful neck awaits a head, either with or without a mustache to illustrate the tale of the local husband who resists his lord's droit du seigneur of deflowering his virgin bride by presenting himself dressed in her costume, mustache and all.

Across from Cosimo, Leonardo merrily completes a female horseman, as he dabs rosettes, a collar, hair pieces, and the horse's tail into place. Someone asks how many of these he completes each day, how long does it take to be finished. "Maybe three" he tosses his head and smiles broadly, "I shouldn't say here with the *padrone* . . ."

Indeed, beside me Francesco bristles. "You should ask me the questions!" he protests, but no one hears him.

"How long did it take you to learn to do this?" Chrysa asks Leonardo.

"Since I was twelve, and I worked here summers, until after I left school and really studied. Then I came here."

After Francesco shows us the ancient wood-fired kiln carved out of the stone hill, we pass carts laden with trays of drying biscuit or unglazed clay plates and bowls and enter the decorating room. Here two men are mixing a pink glaze and dipping enormous garden planters into the liquid. I suspect this will fire to the sienna brown we associate with earthenware, since oxides burn into another hue. Enormous room-size electric kilns are open, one awaiting its load of dried wares already separated by staggers, the other kiln partially emptied but still housing one towering load of rosy *terra cotta* or cooked earthenware. It is cooling, ready to be dipped into glaze, dried, and decorated before returning to the kilns for the final firing. This is the normal routine for all *maioliche* and faience, spanning several days of waiting and processing.

By another entry way sit two decorators. One is scraping the edge of a series of glazed dinner plates with a knife so that the earth color shows through like a brownish border. He brushes on a clear glaze to seal the porous clay. "Your glazes are lead free— *sensa piombo?*" I ask. But of course, he reassures me, it is a non-lead varnish. "We don't use lead any more."

Below, to his right, a wide-eyed child of four sits solemnly at her own decorator's desk. Clad in a plastic apron, she fills a round brush with bright pastel colors from a palette, and blobs abstract patches of paint on a salad dish. Claudio, her apparent mentor, interrupts his work to take a filled plate from her. Wordlessly, he hands her a blank and she intently applies her craft again. Claudio washes off the paints before they dry and puts the plate aside.

"Does she know what you are doing?" I ask Claudio.

"No," he confides, "She thinks they are sold, and when there are no more left, she is happy that the shop has sold everything."

This is Francesco's granddaughter, and I assume this is how all the children in Grottaglie were trained: by their fathers and the gentle artisans of their families' respective workshops. So it was in all the other *fabbricatas* that I knew. Sometimes the children grew happily into the art or business; others left the studio for academic pursuits when they matured.

I hastily cross to Francesco's great shop with its massive display of vases, garden pottery, and horsemen, male and female. *Pupas* large and small, with and without mustaches, garments painted in blue on white. The next room overflows with tableware in colors and designs for every taste and holiday. Next to the traditional dishes with rosettes and blue lines there are rectangular plates in cream with a red antler-like tree in the center. I select a small plate to display next to a similar red design I bought in France. Since the familiar *gallo* appears in all shapes and sizes, I choose a small bowl with hand-pinched handles so I can enjoy the memory of hands molding as well as decorating. A geometric-filled shelf has the same *sgraffito* I'd bought from Enza, whom I was told is the rebellious sister. The location of her shop suggests that she inherited it or was given her shop by father Nicola, for the patriarch usually governs such dispositions of property.

A night later, our group enjoyed a splendid dinner at the Masseria Cantone, a working farm turned glamorous inn, outside the baroque city of Martina Franca. Our table was set with the complete service of the plain creamy provincial pattern with its simple orange edge. Only the service plates had a transfer-printed tree-of-life design. A printed label on the back indicated that the manufacturer was Nicola Fasano at Grottaglie, Italy. Our hostess proudly identified the maker and then pointed out the collection of antique chargers mounted on the walls—all from Grottaglie, all Fasano—a family of talented artists and entrepreneurs whose art survives and thrives.

THE MYSTERY OF MESSAPIA

THOMAS R. HARRELL

"The elephants are dead and the Romans are coming!" So I imagine the fatal news arrived in Hyria (modern Oria), capital of the ancient Messapii people. The Second Punic War between Rome and Carthage was ending, and with it any hope for Puglia's great pre-Roman civilization. For the Messapii had gambled their very survival on Hannibal and his fearsome beasts, and now a victorious Rome was poised to wreak terrible revenge.

I had never heard of the Messapii before traveling to Puglia, but I soon learned that these little-known people built a thriving culture in Puglia that lasted a thousand years before its swift and brutal extinction by the legions of Rome. Little remains of "the first Puglians" today, but as I learned more I became captivated by their rich history. The Messapii, I discovered, will not lie forgotten in their tombs.

Although their demise is no mystery, their origins are shrouded in speculation and myth. Modern scholars generally agree that the Messapii arrived in Puglia between 1500 and 1000 BCE, probably migrating across the Adriatic Sea from Illyria (Albania), but contemporaries of the Messapii offered far more adventurous and romantic ideas of their origins. Closest to modern scholarship was Roman historian Pliny the Elder, who claimed the Messapii descended from nine youths and nine maidens from Illyria. Herodotus, the first Greek historian and "Father of History," wrote that the Messapii descended from Cretans who abandoned that island after the death of King Minos. Some said the Messapii were the sons of weary Trojans escaping the embers of fabled Troy. Still others claimed the Messapii sprang from the children of giants banished by Hercules.

Whatever their true origins, the Messapii soon exploited the riches of the Salentine region of Puglia. Though dismissed by the subsequent Greek settlers of Magna Graecia as "barbarians," the Messapii built thriving city-states throughout southern Puglia, including today's Ostuni, Manduria, Otranto, Brindisi, Ceglie Messapica, and of course Oria. Oria is one of Puglia's five "white cities," so named for their whitewashed splendor rising from the green plains below. An imposing medieval castle built by Frederick II crowns Oria.

From these castle windows I could see Monte Papalucio,

where the Messapii once dedicated a temple to the Greek cult of Demeter and Persephone, goddess symbols of fertility. I wondered if the Messapii, like the Greeks, allowed only women to celebrate the sacred rites of the Mysteries? Did the women cover themselves in flour, honey and oil and celebrate the secret, holy rites with orgiastic dances of mad revelry, twisting and churning their bodies as if possessed? Did other Messapii reject the Greek gods and instead propitiate their own ancient gods at the sacred alter of Egnazia, which, on its own and without fuel, set fire to offerings? Or worship at Pliny's Well, the mysterious well at Manduria where the water level even today never changes whether water is added or drawn?

These mysteries may never be solved. The Messapii language is extinct and few inscriptions remain. Even these are only partially and indefinitely deciphered today. The secrets of the Messapii are well kept indeed.

I did discover that the main occupations of the Messapii were farming (including horses, for which they were famous), trade and war. The well-traveled Pliny the Elder claimed "peerless are the olive groves of the Messapians," and they were the first to cultivate Puglia's *Primitivo* grapes. The Messapii also produced their distinctive *trozzella* pottery (with sharply angled handles and four small wheels on the bottom) for trade within the league of Messapic cities and throughout the region.

No ancient civilization could long survive without skill at war, and the Messapii lived in dangerous proximity to the warlike

Greeks of Magna Graecia. The proudest and most powerful of the Greek city-states in southern Italy, Tarentum (Taranto), host to Plato, Homer, and Virgil, lay just ten miles from Manduria. Conflict was common, which explains why Manduria boasted massive stone walls, built without mortar, thrice encircling the city. Beneath these walls the "barbarian" Messapian army twice inflicted historic defeats on the Greeks, first in 473 BCE when the Messapii destroyed a Greek army (the worst defeat of a Greek army to that date in history), and again in 338 BCE when the Messapii routed the Greeks and killed the Spartan king himself.

But even as the Messapii and Greeks battled for supremacy in Puglia, a new power was rising in Italy. The Roman Republic advanced steadily, inexorably, throughout Italy as its seemingly invincible legions scattered all opposition. The Messapii and their old enemies agreed to unite and together in 280 BCE summoned King Pyrrhus and his army from Greece to confront Rome. King Pyrrhus at first defeated the Romans, but at the cost of so much blood and destruction he lamented that "one more victory like this will be the end of us." Soon after his "pyrrhic victory," he left Italy. With no army capable of resisting Rome, the Messapii chose to submit, and in 266 BCE signed treaties with Rome surrendering their independence and forfeiting Brindisi to the Romans.

For the next fifty years the Messapii lived in uneasy alliance with Rome, autonomous but subservient. Creeping Latinization became the new enemy of Messapian culture and language as

Rome built new cities in Messapia and settled its citizens on the rich farmland. The Messapii appeared helpless to repel Roman encroachment until, in 218 BCE, an irresistible opportunity presented itself in the form of Hannibal Barca.

Raised by his father to hate Rome, Hannibal very nearly toppled his nemesis. His army of Numidians, Libyans, Spaniards and Gauls—with the terrible war elephants—swept from Africa across the Alps, invaded Italy and annihilated one Roman army after another. By 216 BCE Hannibal had crossed the length of Italy to Puglia, where he stopped for food and to encourage rebellion. It was in Puglia that Hannibal won his greatest battle, at Cannae (near present day Foggia), where he came closest to destroying the power of Rome. At the end of that day seventy thousand Roman soldiers and eighty roman senators lay dead or dying on the field. Bodies lay so thick in the Venosa River it was said Hannibal and his men used them as a bridge.

With Rome prostrate, Hannibal's talk of rebellion found ready ears in Messapia. But if Cannae was Hannibal's greatest triumph, it was also among his last. Rome, so nearly broken, recovered. Elephants died, allies deserted or were defeated. Just two years after Cannae, the Roman consul Fabius Maximus and his legions fell upon the rebellious Messapii without mercy. The Messapii could offer little resistance; after years supporting Hannibal's raids, warfare and forage for men and beasts, Messapic cities, villages and farms were near ruin.

I can imagine the treatment of what remained of Messapia

from the fate of Manduria, captured in 209 BCE. The Romans utterly destroyed the city, looting and burning amidst indiscriminate slaughter. Those leading citizens who did not commit suicide were scourged and beheaded; surviving men, women and children were sold into slavery. Vast tracts of land were confiscated by the Roman state and given to loyal allies. Messapia, and its people, disappeared.

Perhaps as the Romans intended, few traces remain of the Messapians' thousand years in Puglia. I found one especially poignant memory of the Messapii at Egnazia, a peaceful place along the Adriatic coast between Bari and Brindisi. The sacred alter is nowhere to be found, and Egnazia today is the site of partially excavated Messapii ditch tombs (intermingled with Greek and Roman tombs and ruins). In these tombs once crouched the Messapii dead. Why crouching, instead of prone like the Romans or Greeks? Another mystery. I like to think it is in anticipation of joining their illustrious ancestors in battle against Hercules, or to avenge the fall of Troy.

Neat fields of thick, timeless olive trees, homage to those who first tilled Puglia's warm earth, planted its olives and vines, and built its cities, surround the Messapian tombs. I walked among the nearby trees and picked one olive. I took it home to plant in the new world, and none will guess its history.

St. Nicholas and My Own Miracle of Bari

Roger Nicholas Webster

*S*t. Nicholas performed many miracles and acts of kindness including rescuing drowning sailors from a stormy sea and, with gift bags of gold, three maidens from a life of prostitution. He lived during the fourth century in Lycia, a part of modern day Turkey. He went on to become the world's most famous man of goodwill and charity—other than those who established major religions. His remains are now in an eleventh century basilica in the heart of Bari, the seaport capital of Puglia, the southeastern most state of Italy. Few non-Europeans know that because of these relics it is one of the significant holy cities of the world.

According to legend, Nicholas was born into an affluent family. He used his wealth to help others. Through a series of incidents that seemed like destiny, he became a Bishop of the

Church, important enough to attend the momentous Council of Nicaea. During the time of Emperor Constantine, this Council literally formulated the tenets of Christianity.

Nicholas died in 342 CE and was buried near where he lived. In 1087, however, when the area was overrun by "infidels" and shortly after the great schism between the Eastern Church based in Constantinople and the Western Church based in Rome, his bones were stolen or rescued—depending on how you look at it—by Baresi fishermen. They brought them back home in triumph where a grand edifice was built for their repose.

How strange that I would find myself in Bari. I was there to join the group of writers working on this book. My connection to St. Nicholas is profound. In Bari, he chose to communicate with me.

I had taken his name as one of my own fourteen years ago when I was chrismated in the Eastern Orthodox Church. My spiritual father told me that since there was no saint bearing the name of Roger, I could choose one and make him my patron. This saint would guide me throughout my life, be available to hear my prayers and intercede on my behalf with God. Especially when I was in the presence of one of his icons or, were I so fortunate, a relic. I could go on about this special connection between the Orthodox and the veneration of their saints, but suffice it to say you either believe or you don't. I was on the fence, searching for confirmation.

I discovered the Church during a time of personal trauma

and spiritual awakening. My mother had died and I needed a sense of belonging. I came from a Protestant background, which for the most part eschewed the idea of saints. Thus, I selected the one I felt closest to and perhaps even shallowly the one who might bring me the most gifts: St. Nicholas, also known as Santa Claus.

Arranging to arrive a day earlier than the rest of the writers, I booked a room in the Palace Hotel, the one nearest the *citta vecchia* (old town). The historic harbor, founded before the Bronze Age, is on a small peninsula jutting into the Adriatic Sea. A modern city of 325,000 people now abuts it.

With a map from the concierge, I set out on my pilgrimage. The area is notorious for the confusing maze of narrow streets. They were paved with large neutral colored stones worn smooth by centuries of traffic. Plants spilled over balconies; small Catholic shrines and banners upon banners of the Italian tricolors—red, green and white—lined the streets.

It was a Saturday. The sounds of families, vendors hawking their wares and ubiquitous motorcycles filled the air. Swallows swooped and sailed above as if they were writing Arabic words in the clear azure sky.

The Castle of Bari was the first landmark. It is a powerful square-towered, Norman structure built by King Roger II in 1132. *A coincidence of name or an omen*, I wondered. Deeper into the warren of streets and corners, I aimed my nose in what I felt was the right direction. The map was useless.

I turned a corner and saw my prize, easily recognizable from its descriptions. Somewhat like a huge limestone barn, it commanded a grand piazza where a crowd of people moved about with anticipation. There was a large door in the center framed by ancient columns that were supported by stone oxen. They were almost unrecognizable with gaping holes where once there were probably horns—of ivory, I fancied. Suddenly, a young bride and groom burst through the portal. As they were being showered with confetti, I spied a side entrance I could use.

Unadorned limestone arches soared to an ornate painted ceiling, where gold baroque framing outlined colorful tableaux. A long red carpet led to an altar covered by a carved stone canopy. Displays of blue agapanthus and white roses, most likely left from the wedding, added elegance. Although perfectly harmonious, it seemed rather empty to me. I noticed a stairway going down; a sign read "The Tomb." That was what I had come to see.

At the bottom of the stairs, I felt an extraordinary sense of peace and reverence. The sound of whispering, the aroma of incense and the cool air soothed my senses. Small windows let in just a few rays of sunlight from the street, which were reflected in the highly polished dark wood pews. People worshipfully tiptoed, kneeled and even prostrated themselves on the rose beige marble floor. A far cry from the whoopla of Santa Claus and his workshop at the North Pole.

Front and center was an area surrounded by iron grillwork.

Here, light from iron chandeliers with candles in red glass shone on an incredibly beautiful and large mosaic icon of St. Nicholas, gently overlaid with a silver cover. Old multi-colored tiles set in geometric patterns decorated the floor. A Maltese cross with a crucified Christ hung over an altar, which was covered by a white, lace-bordered cloth. On it rested vases of perfect white roses and two candle holders made of iron and rock crystal in the form of oxen. The altar covered a space enclosed by a window about four feet long and two feet high.

This was obviously the burial chamber. I bent down to peer inside. A delicately painted mural on the back wall depicted the Saint in his coffin, arms crossed on his breast. It also showed the Holy Hierarch St. Nicolas, the maidens he had rescued, each carrying a small bag of gold coins, and three children in a tub. I felt a shiver go up my spine. My legs tingled.

The Basilica was Roman Catholic, so I did not expect any Orthodox presence. People began to gather around a young, gentle-faced man putting on a black robe behind the screen. Appearing so unusual, I thought for a moment that he might be an intruder, until he began chanting in a Slavic language. Lo and behold, it was to be a short Russian Orthodox service. I was thrilled and participated with heart and soul.

After a personal blessing, many of the celebrants handed the priest pieces of jewelry and small icons, which he placed on the chamber for a few seconds and then returned. I was wearing a very special cross. The year before, I had bought a tiny ancient coin from a Bedouin woman in Petra. In New York, a Chinese friend from Indonesia who is a superb jeweler mounted the coin with a silver Greek cross on the reverse. I preferred to display the cross, so he placed a tiny diamond at its center. I handed the piece to the priest who put it on the reliquary. Passing it back, he gave the cross and me a penetrating look. I was beside myself with joy.

I wear that cross with a sense of amazement and faith. The search, my own personal Miracle of Bari, unfolded like a flower or a series of boxes within boxes. It brought me to the pure spirit of St. Nicholas, now a living presence in my life.

TRULLI, TRULLO

SANDRA BRACKEN

Many years ago, my sculpture studio was in a yurt in Glen Echo Park near Washington, D.C. It was there, in a book on indigenous architecture I first saw photographs of *trulli*. In one picture, a cluster of buildings in the town of Alberobello in the far south of Italy, seemed to be from another planet, luminous in their coat of whitewash. In an aerial view of the countryside, the *trulli* looked like miniature sculptures dotting the landscape. In them I could see the fantasy structures of my childhood—the honeysuckle hut growing in a corner of my grandparents garden and the piles of leaves I raked into leaf houses each fall—and a connection between the dreams of the child and the desires of the adult artist. The *trulli* were visually exciting, somewhat mysterious, and there was an intimate connection between material and place that I felt I already understood. So years later, when in the summer of 2008, I had the opportunity to attend a writers' workshop in Alberobello and live in a *trullo* for ten days, no wonder I said "Yes." From the day of my decision, the rhythm of *trulli trullo, trulli trullo* played continuously in my head like a siren song.

I had to suspend my excitement and anticipation momentarily to consider the posssibility of being disillusioned. It happens. It happens when you've been carrying an image in your head for so long—thirty years. It becomes idealized; embellished to the point of a perfected, and protected idea. I had to remember that I found inspiration in the *trullo* form partly because of its raison d'etre: using a material that is close at hand for construction, in the most direct way, to build a substantial structure. It just so happened, that in the process, a form both beautiful and utilitarian evolved. Had it survived the test of time?

For practical information I returned to my original source, *The Prodigious Builders* by Bernard Rudofsky. A *trullo*, the plural is *trulli*, is a traditional dwelling unique to the area of Valle d'Itria in Puglia. Constructed of local limestone, they were historically dry-laid, that is without mortar. The first circle of stone was laid directly on the ground. Successive layers were placed on top in concentric circles.

There are several stories about why no mortar was originally used. The most interesting was about avoiding the taxes on permanent structures. When the revenue collector was en route, the buildings were easily, and quickly, dismantled. When he arrived he found only a pile of stones. Over time mortar was used in their construction with a cone shaped roof sitting on a low square base. Many have a rounded finial on top. This roof, I think, is a *trullo's* most distinctive feature: the breast-like form dominates the structure.

In some, the design became a bit more complex; walls consisted of an inner and outer layer. The space in between was filled with smaller stones. Many were covered completely with a layer of whitewashed cement. Side rooms were added as families grew. Completed *trulli* were connected, creating larger extended living spaces.

Walking into Alberobello the first time, I discovered a new meaning for the expression "urban sprawl": It was difficult to tell where one *trullo* ended and another began. There were hundreds of them. There was no way a single photograph could show them all. As I walked up via San Marco to my *trullo*, I passed several that had been converted into shops and restaurants. I knew beforehand that I would not have a specific idea of interior space from photographs or from Rudofsky's drawings. He had written "no two interiors are alike." Needless to say, I was curious about the inside of mine. From the street, the typical *trullo* shape was not visible.

Disappointed, I entered through one of the double doors set in an ordinary rectangular wall that opened into the larger of two side rooms. This was the kitchen; charming, but not what I expected. I had to walk through an arched opening to reach the domed central space, the heart of the *trullo*. It defined the largest interior room which functioned as a bedroom. The stone floor measured twelve feet by twelve feet. Walls extended seven feet high, where the inward curve of the dome began. The walls were punctuated by arched openings and smaller alcoves or niches. I had read that the niches were used as sleeping spaces for children. But they would have been very small. The earthy pink limestone was lightly whitewashed giving a decorated warmth to the room. It would have been dark and forbidding if another type of stone had been used. The well-worn surfaces of the uneven stones softened their overall appearance. It seemed natural to want to look up, to look into the dome twenty feet above.

Despite the height, the space felt cozy: the stone created a sense of quiet enclosure, a feeling that it was a safe place. The very tiny window just below the apex of the dome was unusual.

On the first morning I woke to a faint glow above—a nice surprise. Gentle light gradually washed over the curve of the dome beginning at the top. The intensity of light changed as the movement of the sun changed. Another surprise was how the light of the full moon warmed the deep darkness of night. To my best reckoning that little window faced east. After awhile, I decided I could tell time from that built-in "sundial."

In the countryside surrounding Alberobello, I saw individual *trullo* scattered in fields, some partially dismantled. Piles of stones lying on the ground next to one reminded me of the ancient tax man. Others were completed structures without mortar, stucco or paint, most likely used for storage. These were like the first photographs I had seen. I could see them individually as sculpture; I understood how symbolic the *trulli* image and idea had been. It was where I could see myself playing.

For my sculpture in the intervening years, instead of stones I gathered sticks, vines and reeds, the materials in the woods and marshes near where I lived. I used cement too, but in a wattle and daub fashion. Perhaps if stones had been lying around, my pieces would have had an entirely different look.

On the morning of the summer solstice, I left the *trullo* at five and walked up the hill to a vacant lot with a good view of the eastern horizon. The sky over Alberobello was filled with swallows—I like to think they were keen to join me in welcoming the longest day of the year.

My ideal vision of this place did not include the many thousands of *trulli* that are in Puglia—the renovated ones, the newly built as homes, the miniature mementoes and *trulli* key chains. In recent years, the area has become increasingly popular as a tourist attraction. *Trulli* are also used as hotels. Does that take away from their integrity or their historical significance or my own experience of them? They are still visually appealing, all of them, old and new. And obviously they are quite functional. Thankfully, the area is a World Heritage site and protected: building regulations have to adhere to UNESCO regulations. I think I expected only a few protected historical buildings, more of them in the country than in town. I never thought the *trulli* would or could be a viable part of the twenty-first century.

Experiencing them now, the *trulli* seemed to belong exactly where they were. The presence of so much limestone in the area and much of it lying in piles on the ground, gave them the appearance that they were a form that grew out of the earth, a natural extension of a rocky landscape. I find the logic of the way they came into being reassuring. It was the challenge that drove my desire to make sculpture—to use a naturally occurring material, something close at hand, that when simply rearranged could create a form that stimulated imagination, perhaps even a deeper inward journey. Now that I have had the experience of living in a *trullo*, I know that for me it rightly embodies past and present.

Being under the dome was magical, filled with innocence and the memories of a childhood leaf house. Encompassed in that space was possibility, an invitation and approval to be a part of the creative process beyond those walls. Piles of stones, piles of leaves can become more than what they seem.

TIME TRAVEL

NANCY ALPERT

*P*eople change over thirty years, right? That's why I figured a writers' workshop in Italy would be an enhanced version of my first forays overseas. At eighteen, I toured Europe with a high school group and at age twenty, I returned to Italy for a six-month junior year abroad. Back then, I was often homesick, reserved (read "prudish") and tentative. I traveled student-class, with hoards of other bargain hunters. This time, I was flying first class for the first time in my life—a mileage point reward for years of credit card purchases and an expensive divorce. Surely my first big trip since the birth of my daughter seven years ago would be The Triumphant Return of the New Nancy approaching mid-life with more life.

Or would it?

Under the hot sun of the Graeco-Messapian ruins of Egnazia,

near Monopoli, I had an insight about how some things do not change over the years. For instance, I still did not have the patience for piles of rocks, or a delight for dates in history. I still could not keep track of the endless cycle of civilizations and the long list of conquerors and the archeological ruins they left in their wake.

The museum at Egnazia exhibited relics, from the Bronze Age to the Middle Ages, from settlements along the Adriatic coast, as well as mosaic floors from Roman Taranto mansions. Painted figurations from *trozzelle*, earthenware vessels found in chamber tombs, illustrate aspects of life in the third and fourth centuries BCE. I was drawn to a panel that portrays a young man, dressed in a red tunic and a yellow mantle lined with azure, holding the reins of a horse.

What piqued my imagination were not only the remnants of people's lives—the tools they used, their ceramic pottery and creative artwork, but the items they carefully chose to put in tombs to assist the dead on their journey beyond. Children's graves contained food, toys and clothes, while adult sites contained food, jewelry and make-up.

As a mom, my heart ached for the tiny burial victims and the parents who had to place them in their graves. As a social worker to seniors, I have often thought about the cycle of life and mortality. Life is ultimately very short. Most of us try to pack in happiness, love and meaning amidst inevitable suffering and loss. But what do we leave behind when we die? And what do we take with us? I hope to enter the next world with a more evolved soul, and I hope to leave this world better off than when I entered it. My legacy will likely be through my work, small acts of human kindness and the gift of my daughter.

Standing in the ancient necropolis of Egnazia, I let myself wonder what items I would want in my grave to aid me in the next life. I would leave behind the decorative art, the fine china, the hair pins and combs. My list would include:

- A versatile travel outfit to dress up or down, depending on the occasion.
- Jewelry. I'd bring a few pieces that honor the mother/daughter relationship.
- Make-up—centuries of women couldn't be all wrong!
- A few samples of awards I've won, letters from people I've helped, and love notes received from family and friends—a kind of resume from this life to show to interested parties in the next.
- A few good books and some knitting, just in case I am in "limbo" for awhile.

Dwelling on the past and thinking about family and legacies, I walked back into the museum and called my daughter. We didn't talk about the relics found in the burial tombs of ancient children. We talked about ice cream. She told me she'd eaten gelato in my honor and asked if I'd run into any princesses in any castles we'd visited.

"No, no princesses yet," I said.

"But I did have some delicious gelato at Pookie's Gelateria in Matera," I continued. "They had tray after tray of ice-cream with pretty fruit slices on top that reminded me of the fruit plates you design for grandma and grandpa. They all looked so yummy that I couldn't decide which flavors to order—so I chose a berry flavor (*mirtillo*) and a chocolate chip (*stracciatella*) in your honor."

In many ways, I have changed and so has Italy. Thirty years ago, I ate tons of gelato just for myself. This trip, I ate little, but I was eating for two. Today, throughout Italy there is a decrease in smoking, honking and parking on sidewalks. No longer did I have to eat my pasta in a pall of cigarette smoke—the prohibition against smoking in bars and restaurants was surprisingly well-observed in most Puglian restaurants. And I was so shocked by the patience of the drivers in southern Italy that I kept asking our tour bus driver if there were new anti-honking laws that explained the silence. Thirty years ago, sidewalks were like narrow jigsaw puzzles of cars jammed every which way.

In Bari, the capital of Puglia, it was a pleasure to walk unencumbered down the sidewalks to do my window-shopping. And I do mean window-shopping. With the introduction of the euro in 2002 and the poor exchange rate in the summer of 2008, I wasn't doing much buying. I definitely felt wealthier with three thousand lira burning a hole in my pocket than with a paltry two-euro coin.

Thirty years ago I loved, ate, and prayed my way across Italy.

In 2008, the workshop's itinerary did not leave much time to cultivate a romance. I certainly ate well—Puglian cuisine is amongst the finest in Italy. And I pray to return soon with my daughter.

On the Road, Without the Band

Carol J. Kelly

Violenza, crimini e povertà
Fannu parte te la quotidianità
Mentre ci allu governu te sta società
Face te tuttu cu ne scunne la realtà

Violence, crime and poverty
Are part of our daily lives
While the government of this society
Hides this reality from us

—Sud Sound System
Violenza, Crimini e Povertà (Violence, Crime and Poverty)

*O*f all the places to find a local reggae band, Salento in Italy's southern region of Puglia seemed unlikely. Sud Sound System's rich rhythms, heavy on bass and percussion, reminded me of the music I grew up listening to—and, of course, dancing to—in Jamaica. Though I knew some Italian, I didn't understand their songs because the lyrics were in Salento dialect.

Sud Sound System's energetic music recalled the lively, fast-paced style of dancehall, a subgenre of reggae that was popular in the 1980s, and popularized by singers like Shinehead, Ninja Man, and Beenie Man. It also brought me way, way back to bands like Toots and the Maytals, Bob Marley and the Wailers, and to singers like John Holt, Gregory Isaacs and U-Roy who were among my favorites when I was hanging out with school friends in Kingston. Reggae and even its precursors—ska and rock steady—are ingrained in my sense memory.

Back then, the music was a constant soundtrack to my daily life. Even today, all over the island in towns like Portmore, where I visit my aunt on frequent trips from New York, loudspeakers still blast reggae every night into the wee hours.

I first stumbled on Sud Sound System in an Italian guidebook while preparing for a writing workshop in Puglia, the "heel" of Italy's "boot." The whole notion of a big southern reggae scene and a band from Salento was intriguing. *Why here?* I wondered. As well, I was fascinated by Sud Sound System's highly political message along with their stubborn decision to sing in local dialect, which could be lost in translation even for native Italians from other regions. Similarly, most Jamaican reggae groups sing in patois, the vocabulary of the island's poor, from whom this style of socially conscious music emerged in the late 1960s.

Band leader Nandu Popu told the guidebook's authors about the influence of his local language: "The dialect is an antidote. It's the antidote to the sickness of our society caused by stress, ambition and superficiality, and the idea that anything is acceptable in the name of money." He said southern dialect captures "the rhythm of nature," the sea and the land. The singer cited the link between reggae and the desire to express the aspirations of people "forgotten and exploited by progress."

What was it about the Italian south and Jamaica? Perhaps history had acted on people and cultures over five thousand miles apart in very similar ways, enabling this dance to the same rhythm. Italy's south suffered the kind of economic hardship common to so-called Third World countries like Jamaica. Puglia's struggles with underdevelopment, high unemployment, emigration, crime and the Mafia's chokehold were topics addressed by Sud Sound System. And reggae has long been critical of social injustice and a system of government that saps poor people. *What else did Italy's rural south and Jamaica have in common? I wondered. Why was Salento called la Jamaica Italiana?* Perhaps reggae resonated with people who felt alienated, beaten down and left behind. Perhaps the connection was more mysterious. Still, I set out to explore the path that led to musical kinship, and to understand—at least in part—why the vast farmlands of Puglia provided fertile soil for reggae to flourish.

There's a saying that a language is a dialect with an army and a navy. It's no surprise that official Italian is the Tuscan dialect of the rich and powerful north. The dialects of Puglia, made up of Greek, Latin, Arabic and Spanish words, tell the story of the south in words its occupiers left behind. These words echo the region's bitter history of invasions, starting from the eighth century BCE when the Greeks founded a string of settlements along the Ionian coast.

Jamaica had its own share of occupiers, starting with the Spanish in 1494, to English colonial rule that began in 1655. The bitter history of slavery left its economic and cultural imprint. And patois, a blend of English and African words not spoken at the dinner table when I was a child, is widely used by reggae artists.

As I listened to Sud Sound System's music on YouTube and got help translating their lyrics, I found another theme the band shared with or borrowed from Jamaican reggae groups—the importance of staying true to cultural roots. In fact, "roots reggae" is a subgenre that honors African culture and the Rastafari movement—the spiritual underpinnings of many popular Jamaican musicians.

Se nu te scierri mai delle radici ca tieni
Rispetti puru quiddre delli paisi lotanti!
Se nu e scierri mai de du ede ca ieni
Dai chiu valore alla cultura ca tieni!

If you don't forget your roots
You respect the ones of countries far from yours!
If you don't forget your roots
You value your culture more!

—SUD SOUND SYSTEM
La Radici Ca Tieni (The Roots That You Have)

Two weeks after discovering the band, I was in Puglia's gritty capital of Bari enjoying a summer *passeggiata* (evening stroll) on the narrow, labyrinthine alleyways of the old city that dated back thirty-five hundred years. Young people, families with children and couples were walking about, stopping in cafes and *gelaterie* (ice cream parlors). Old women sat in doorways, reminding me of the elderly ladies who would sit on verandas in rural villages of Jamaica. I was careful as I walked around because I had been warned that like Kingston, Jamaica's capital, Bari had a reputation for crime. The old city's vibrant street life, with its fish and vegetable stands and people socializing outdoors, stirred childhood memories. The next morning, I felt a gentle breeze as I walked along the coast in the hot sun and came upon a group of local fishermen with low-tech boats and equipment—not unlike a scene from any Caribbean coastal community. The sea, the sun, the land and the laid-back lifestyle all resonated with me.

Weeks earlier, on the band's Web site, I was thrilled to find out that one of their concert dates was June eighteenth in Bari during the first week of my trip. I wasn't sure exactly how close Puglia's capital was to Alberobello, the small *trulli* town where our travel group would be staying, but I was sure of one thing: I would find a way to go.

Two days before the concert, we visited the band's beautiful hometown of Lecce, called the Florence of the south because of its unique baroque style of architecture. There, I had one of those so-near-yet-so-far experiences. My only contact with the band was Francesca, the girlfriend of Andrea Moretti, a travel adviser I met at the Italian Tourist Office in Manhattan. It was *una fortunata coincidenza* (a lucky coincidence) that she also lived in Lecce and knew someone who knew someone in the band. With our local guide Marilù as interpreter, Francesca encouraged me to contact her friend Marinazzo, who later gave me a number for the band's studio.

On the morning of the concert, I felt light and excited. As we boarded our tour bus, Marilù said there might be a snag. My heart plummeted. I trusted Marilù, a thoughtful, pretty and highly professional young woman from Bari; I expected her to have good hometown sources.

This being Italy, the concert was indeed canceled, with no

explanation. And after weeks of anticipation, I was crushed.

Meanwhile, I kept calling the band's studio (no answer), surfing the Internet for their songs, and talking to Alberobello locals about reggae. I also started searching for someone to translate Salento dialect, which turned out to be a tall order.

On my last day in Italy—a few hours before heading for the airport—I went into Centro Musica, a record store on Bari's bustling Corso Vittorio Emanuele. There, I bought *Dammene Ancora* (Give Me More), which is Sud Sound System's latest CD. Store owner Vito Causarano said Sud Sound System was the most popular local reggae band, but there were others. In an email a few weeks later, Vito wrote, in Italian, that reggae was very widespread in the 1970s, thanks to artists of the calibre of Bob Marley, Peter Tosh and Dennis Brown. "Southern Italy has taken in many of these sounds, making them their own," he continued, adding that the rhythm in southern folk music like *pizzica* or *taranta* are close enough to the rhythmic cadences of reggae. Vito attributed Sud Sound System's success to "the freshness of their sounds and to the lyrics that are very tied to social realities." He cited Nidi d'Arac, Mascarimiri, Radicanto and Etnoritmo as popular bands that sing mainly traditional music. Besides Sud Sound System, other reggae bands of note included Treble, Marina & Papa Leu, Boom da bash and Rankin Lele.

Mafia bussiness controlla l'Italia
Mafia bussiness controlla la miseria

Mafia business controls Italy
Mafia business controls misery

—Sud Sound System
T'a Sciuta Bona (You Got Away With It)

My quest for a translator revealed some quirks Italians and Jamaicans have in common. A wonderful travel manager at our *trulli* resort promised to put me in touch with a colleague who spoke Salento dialect. I emailed her several times and called her office from Brooklyn, but she never got back to me. Like Italians, Jamaicans are rarely forthcoming when asked a favor. You usually get a breezy "yeah, man," then there's no follow-through. And Jamaicans, like Italians, are always late, never rushed, and possess a mellow, "no problem" approach to life.

A month after my trip to Puglia, I was finally on the phone with Sud Sound System's band leader. One of Francesca's friends, Dario Quarta, a journalist for a magazine called *quiSalento*, knew Nandu personally.

"It was an instinctive choice," said Nandu, when I asked why his band sang in dialect. He was animated and passionate as he continued in Italian. "From way back in our school days," said Nandu, the band members were proud of their identity and of

Salento dialect and culture. The group of three on-stage members has been together since 1987, and their first recording was in 1991. *Dammene Ancora* was the band's twelfth CD. Nandu said they chose reggae because of the south's "similarities with Jamaica and Africa." Southern Italy is geographically close to Africa, added Nandu, "and Puglia has more in common with Tunisia and Morocco than with northern Europe."

Nandu said his music was heavily influenced by mento, an outdated, fast-paced style of Jamaican folk music considered the grandfather of reggae. Though the band had never been to Jamaica, Nandu "would love to collaborate with Jamaican artists." He hoped "to bring Sud Sound System's music throughout the world, and to try different styles of reggae."

I asked Nandu why the concert in Bari was canceled. His only response was, "I don't know. It wasn't our fault." Later, in an email, he said: "The organizers decided to change the date and location but didn't inform our agency," adding, "This is the Italian f——— way!" Then he invited me to Salento for the August *festa* (festival).

What Nandu said about Italy's proximity to Africa got me thinking about race in reference to Italians and a recent *Wall Street Journal* article on the definition of whiteness, by June Kronholz: "Whiteness and the privileges that came with it were so closely guarded that in 1912, a House committee held hearings on whether Italians were really Caucasian," said Thomas Guglielmo, a historian at George Washington University. The idea was picked up from Italy, where northern, lighter-skinned Italians were asking the same questions about the southern, darker-skinned Italians, continued the article.

To be sure, this idea has long been debunked, but I wondered if an old perception of southerners factored into reggae's popularity in the region.

Musical influences often cross borders, building bridges across language. I felt proud that in less than forty years, an original music genre whose birth I witnessed had been adopted all over the world. The rhythms of a small island in the Caribbean Sea echoed in a region washed by the Ionian and Adriatic Seas.

Though I didn't get to see or hear the band, I heard and felt the pulse of the south as I traveled throughout Salento—to such towns as Brindisi, Oria, Ostuni, Grottaglie and Martina Franca. I explored Sud Sound System's cultural roots. As well, I deepened my appreciation of reggae and my own Jamaican heritage as I replayed the songs of my youth. Music, like travel, reveals how strikingly similar we all are.

TENUTE AL BANO CARRISI: PUGLIA'S GRACELAND

DENISE ALTOBELLO

*T*scoop up a handful of olive leaves and stash them into my new Italian bra. Who would have thought that my Monday lunch in Brindisi would be hosted by Italy's own version of the king of rock 'n' roll? But here I am, at age fifty-three, collecting souvenir plunder from the grounds of Tenute Al Bano Carrisi just as I did forty-five years ago in front of the guitar-marked gates of Graceland. But this time, I am invited in by Puglia's own king, Al Bano Carrisi—farmer, singer, actor and father. And new bra or not, my shallow soul shivers in anticipation.

Sipping a tiny cup of thick black espresso in Tenute Carrisi's gourmet restaurant, I scan the photographs, news clippings and framed *Volare* album covers adorning the walls and giggle, "Kind of like Graceland, isn't it?" My lunch partners laugh in agreement that the restaurateur certainly appears to be more than a bit taken with his own celebrity. What I keep to myself, however, is that my groupie sensibility is completely at home in this super-charged shrine to self-congratulation. Darn! Even Pope John Paul deigned to smile for the camera when Al Bano shook his hand. Who is this guy? The Italian Tom Jones? Puglia's Presley?

Buongiorno! In the sunlit entry of the dining room, a short, sturdy man dressed in the uniform black shirt of southern Italy beams a smile at our group and announces that he, Al Bano Carrisi and not his assistant, will give us a tour of his five hundred hectare estate.

Yes! I think. *Once I figure out exactly who Al Bano is, I can add him to my brag sheet.*

Relishing his role as lord of the manor, Al Bano barks an indecipherable order to a hapless assistant and leads us out into the sunlight. He tells us that this section of Puglia was once called Little America until the 1990s when President Clinton closed the American NATO base in nearby San Vito dei Normanni. Powerful arms point with pride to a thousand-year-old olive tree whose roots have endured despite the sometimes-painful history of the oft-besieged province of Brindisi. Never one to ignore a talisman or a souvenir, I pluck a few of its leaves and stash them in my bosom as Al Bano directs us through the olive trees to the vineyard that supplies his winery with the *Primitivo* and *Negro Amaro* grapes that are the signature of Puglia. Hearing that several in our entourage hail from California, he chuckles, "Sorry, Francis Ford Coppola, but I think my wine is better."

I may not have heard of this man before today, but I sure do like his style, I think.

"Our first bottling was in 1973." He displays a bottle of Salento Don Carmelo. "It was named to honor my father. The second was named for Plato." He lifts the bottle of Platone Salento.

"Plato?"

"*Si*. He was the first to write about wine, *no*? And this area was part of Magna Graecia, *si*?"

Just then, the sound of rushing water emerges from around a stone wall topped by ancient olive jars. We arrive at a small lake bound on one end by an impressive manmade waterfall and on the other by a trio of tiny brown horses.

"Not Elvis's guitar-tiled swimming pool, but maybe a touch of Neverland," I crack.

"That one is Francescero. Named for the last king of the Empire of the Two Sicilies." Al Bano smiles affectionately at one of the horses. "And that one is the Heretic." His gaze falls on another. Sensing our surprise with his devotion to philosophy and history, he explains, "I was a schoolteacher for two years. Then I found my way in the music."

And find his way he did. Al Bano left his home in Puglia's Colline San Marco as a teenager and made his debut in 1966 at Italy's La Festival delle Rose. In 1967, he recorded the hit *Nel*

Sole and toured with the Rolling Stones in Italy. By 1970, he married his *Nel Sole* co-star, Romina Power, singer-daughter of Hollywood heartthrob, Tyrone Power, and the first of their four children, Ylenia Maria Sole, was born.

Both the schoolteacher and pop culture queen in me warm toward our flamboyant host, and I decide that a few oleander blossoms from his lush gardens might be a fragrant addition to my cache of Carrisi memorabilia. I pluck one of the vanilla-scented double blooms and tuck it alongside the olive leaves.

Standing in front of a one-story stucco and stone building, Al Bano tells us that this ground, where the farm's wheat and chaff are separated, is holy to him. So, he built this chapel presided over by two statues, fruit of his fifteen year search after they disappeared from the ruins of his childhood church. Today, Santo Giovanni and the Madonna appear quite at home within their glass wall niches in this rustic and sunlit chapel.

Again, I wonder. The chapel, the quest for the statues, the viticultural homage to patriarchs and philosophers. Are these devotions sincere or are they prideful manifestations of the provincial boy made good? I think of Elvis's behemoth airplane, the Lisa Marie—The Flying Graceland. Hmph! Who am I to judge? What about me at Graceland? I wasn't really an Elvis fan at such a young age, but I was really eager to show off the Elvis leaf collection to Moo-Moo, Lil' Tater and the other kids on my street who never traveled farther than the boundaries of our New Orleans Ninth Ward neighborhood. *Why should Al Bano demur about his accomplishments*, I wonder, slipping a sprig of mint into the recesses of my ambitious bra.

"*Popi!*" Two small children call from a playground littered with toys and equipment. Al Bano beams and reaches down to squeeze the little boy to his chest before walking us through part of his private residence. Photographs of both generations of his six children smile from nearly every surface. We enter the one-time *forno* (wood burning oven) converted into a recording studio decorated with many of his twenty-six gold and eight platinum records. His dark eyes gleam as he points to the framed clippings from his months on tour with The Rolling Stones, his concerts for Pope John Paul II and his stand-in performances for Luciano Pavarotti in *The Three Tenors*.

We settle in for a farewell toast in the low-ceilinged bar adjacent to the studio. Champagne corks pop and golden bubbles fill our flutes. Al Bano decides that the time has come for a private concert. His rousing rendition of *Volare* ends with cheers and laughter. I squeeze into a space at the bar and introduce myself.

He returns my greeting. "*Piacere.* You are a writer, yes?"

"Sometimes, yes."

He asks about my Italian surname. "Altobello," he chuckles. "Tall and handsome, yes?"

I laugh. "That's what I hear. Except the Altobellos come from the land of the short people in Sicilia. What about your name? What does Al Bano mean?"

"Albano. For Albania. My father was there with the Italian

army when I was born in 1943. My mother wanted to honor him in that way." Yet again, I am seduced by his devotion to the roots of family and history.

"Where are you from, Signora Altobello?"

"New Orleans."

"A sad story, New Orleans." He averts his glance and rubs at a wet spot on the olive wood bar.

I sigh; weary of—but ready for—the well-intentioned questions about Katrina. "It was, but things are improving. We're coming back."

"My daughter Ylenia—she went missing in New Orleans many years ago."

Seconds pass before I hazard the question. "Did you find her?"

"No, we did not."

Later I learned that Ylenia, the letter-turner on Italy's *Wheel of Fortune*, left Puglia to pursue the life of a novelist in New Orleans. She disappeared there in January of 1994. One witness claimed to have seen her dive into the Mississippi River. Police reports in New Orleans provide no definitive answers about her fate, but Elvis-like sightings often surface in European tabloids. Al Bano's biography, *E La Mia Vita*, written with Alberto Allegri, reveals his own acceptance that Ylenia is not alive. Most poignant are his words: "I can tell my story . . . of happiness and also of profound sadness . . . I am not immune from either." But like the scarred thousand-year-old olive tree, Al Bano not only endures, he thrives.

On this sunny June day in Puglia, Al Bano turns and graciously toasts his visiting band of writers: "Today, I am happy for two reasons. One, *cuzza* you come. And two, this is like . . . when Americans [from the NATO base] were in this place all the time."

Amid a chorus of *grazie, arrivederci*, we make our way back through the garden. He orders the assistant to bring us CDs and brochures for Tenute Al Bano Carrisi. Chastened, yet admiring, I stash these final souvenirs into my purse and climb aboard the bus back to Alberobello. The scent of oleander and mint wafts from my bra, and I smile down at the damp olive leaves sticking to my skin. No, I decide, not just like Graceland. But clearly full of grace.

Extra-Virgin

Connie Gutowsky

On the drive to Lecce our guide, Marilù, tan in slim white jeans, zippered tee and sparkling sandals, stands at the front of the tour-bus, microphone in hand, and offers insights about what we see out the windows: vineyards, artichokes, tall stalks of wheat turning gold, almond trees and fennel with feathery ferns. Dry, rough walls of limestone separate fields of olive trees in this rich agricultural region.

These revered trees can live for centuries even under harsh conditions and neglect, able to sprout new growth when trimmed and watered. Their whorls, as gnarled as my own arthritic hands, still turn heads. Northern Italians come to Brindisi to take thou-sand-year-old trees, roots and all, to decorate their villas, we are told. The Pugliese have had to enact laws to protect their local treasures.

For thousands of years the ripe plump promise, the olive, brought hope to Puglia in the sensuous form of oil. It nourished as food in cooking and flavoring. The oil brought light in lamps. It annointed bodies in athletic competitions and in the ceremonial last rites when dying. It brought luster to skin and hair. It promoted health. The oil was so dominant, it became a form of currency and wealth.

Here, olive trees are everywhere. They grow in well-tended groves, bare earth beneath the rows of trees. Slanting light plays with their leaves, whose patina varies from gray-green to silver. They grow in family gardens, large planter boxes and clay pots on village streets and squares, fifty million in all. The cultivation of olives remains one of Puglia's finest and most reliable economic resources.

During and before feudal times, Puglia, a place of harsh sun and parched land, could not support a herd of cows, or even many pigs or chickens. Olive trees, however, thrive in such a climate. The fruit ripens between October and December when the inside color varies between green and purple, with flavors of almond, grass and cherry. In past times, peasants picked and cured the olives, or pitted them with a knife and pressed them with a mortar and pestle at home or in the communal town press. Both were laborious processes. Today, the picking and pressing of olives are done by machines which wash them, remove the fruit from any twigs or branches, and extract oil. The more abundant production is shared throughout the world, and the cold pressed extra-virgin olive oil produced in Puglia is highly prized.

Whether young or old, people benefit from extra-virgin olive oil. It is good for the brain. It prevents heart disease, strokes and arteriosclerosis. Aerobics in a spoon? Doctors beam when they reveal it minimizes osteoporosis and cellular aging, diabetes and various kinds of cancer. Extra-virgin olive oil stars in the Mediterranean diet, one of the healthiest in the world. Generous use is made of cold-pressed extra-virgin olive oil for salads, for seasoning pasta and bread, for frying and baking vegetables, meats and fish. For me the magic of the olive and olive oil has always been the taste.

Today the cuisine of Puglia is considered one of the finest in Italy. Chatting with Marilù about local cooking, I learn that for *cena* (dinner), her mother prepares five ounces of pasta per person. In summer, the pasta might be *orecchiette* with fresh tomato sauce and fresh basil, seasoned with a local cold-pressed extra-virgin olive oil. It might be served with a small piece of lamb, a plate of chicory topped with lemon slices surrounded by thin rounds of zucchini, a glass of *Primitivo* wine and fresh peaches for *dolce* (dessert).

While most of the time my roommate, Ethel, and I dined out, we twice cooked Puglian-style in our essential Italian kitchen, which contained one pasta pan, a medium-size sauce pan, a small cup-like pan to heat milk, cheese-grater, large perforated spoon and sharp knife. On our first day here, Ethel had stocked our pantry with a small bottle of local cold-pressed extra-virgin olive oil, *orecchiette*, tomatoes and ripe red cherries.

A few days later we decided to visit the local grocer at the top of the hilly lane. Leaving home, we opened our front door, pushed aside the row of hanging amber beads which rustled like autumn leaves, stepped into our tiny garden, heavy with the scent of rosemary. Two cat-friends dozed in the sun near red geraniums. We pushed open our gate after lifting the rope that secured it, picket to post. From the grocer we brought mixed vegetables, a lemon and a cantaloupe-size sweet cucumber. The sun was bright, tomatoes were ripe, and we tore fresh basil and bread to dunk in extra-virgin olive oil, stirred with salt and pepper. We made a salad which included fennel, radish, a splash of cold pressed extra-virgin olive oil, a squeeze of lemon and a grind of pepper, just enough to please the palate, not enough to pad the paunch. We set our table with flatware from the drawer beneath the red-and-white-checked table cloth and within minutes ate a healthy supper.

A famous Italian singer said, "In the kitchen you are always in good voice." We didn't sing as we cooked, though we were happy enough to have done so.

MUSSELS FARMING
IN TARANTO

BARBARA J. EUSER

At the Hotel Ristorante Orsa Maggiore near Santa Cesarea, I sampled *Cozze d'Otranto*; at L'Ancora Ristorante near Monopoli, the mussels were served *all'Ancora* over tagliolini in a rich sauce with clams and shrimp; at Don Carmelo's Ristorante Pizzeria in Alberobello, the mussels were served in a casserole. It seemed every restaurant in Puglia had its own favorite—and delectable—way of preparing mussels.

I have eaten mussels elsewhere in Europe. In Brussels, Belgium, I have eaten mounds of steamed mussels in a delicately flavored broth served with crisp French fries. On Ile de Re in France, I have eaten them in a creamy curry sauce. In Neapolis, Greece, I have eaten them on the half shell, baked with cheese and tomatoes.

But the plumpest, juiciest, most succulent mussels I have ever tasted were in Puglia. As a mussel aficionado, I had to learn more about these exceptional examples of my favorite shellfish, *Mytilus galloprovincialis*.

It was no great surprise to learn that the largest mussel farm in Italy is in Taranto, producing about twelve thousand tons of mussels per year. According to one source, "The Mar Piccolo of Taranto represents a pattern of enclosed coastal marine ecosystem in which the intense activity of mussel culture makes it the most important mussel farming [location] in Italy."

Taranto is a port city located on the Ionian Sea on the western coast of Puglia. On the inner edge of the Mar Grande of Taranto, there is a narrow opening leading to the Mar Piccolo, a lagoon that is itself divided into two basins, the Primo Seno and the Secundo Seno. A total of thirty-four freshwater springs, as well as several small rivers, feed into Mar Piccolo, diluting the sea water that enters from the Mar Grande. Mussels thrive in this semi-saline solution.

Taranto, known as Taras by its original Greek settlers, then as Tarentum by it Roman rulers, has been renowned for mussel production for twenty-five centuries. Pliny and Virgil referred to the mussels of Taras in their writings. Documents dating from 1204 to 1395 indicate that the Roman Catholic Church, recognizing the commercial importance of mussels, had laid claim to certain fishing rights. By the fifteenth century, the industry was important enough to be regulated by fishing laws inscribed in the *Libro Russo*, the *Directorium Dohanaarum Rubrum*, of the Taranto princes.

The earliest Greek settlers picked mussels up out of the mud in the shallow waters of the Mar Piccolo. They discovered how to use tree branches to create rakes with long tines, which they used to rake mussels together into mounds. They shoveled the mounds of mussels into baskets to carry home or to sell.

Although mussels may grow unattached in the sea bed, they prefer to attach themselves to something—a rock, stick or piece of rope. In the sixteenth century, Giovine described mussel tilling techniques. In the seventeenth century, Giannattasio described a special technique used to farm mussels that involved half-burying *bouchòts* (pine stakes) in the sea bed. According to Giannattasio, a crusader stopped in Taranto on his return from the Middle East, learned the technique and passed it on to mussel fisherman throughout Europe.

In the sixteenth and seventeenth centuries, mussel production reached a new level. Fishermen established their first cooperatives in an attempt to free themselves from the commercial control of the Roman Catholic Church and local lords. Data from a land registry of 1746 shows a total of 493 fishermen and 19 tenants of mussel fishing grounds.

In the second half of the eighteenth century, mussel farmers discovered that mussels would firmly attach themselves to the fibers of a lightly woven rope. They developed a system that employed *zoche* (cane ropes) specially spun by a rope maker using an iron wheel called in local dialect *la rota ti lu fiskalaru*. Mussel farmers tied the *zoche* to stakes which were anchored in the fishing ground, the stake tops reaching upwards through the water's surface like outstretched arms. Farmers hung mussels in the ropes, weaving them in pairs into the *zoche*. The young mussels grew suspended in their *zoche* from October to April, when they were fully grown and could be harvested and sold.

During the reign of King Ferdinando II di Borbone from 1810-1859, productive water properties were divided up between feudal lords and religious orders.

In 1900, Augustus J.C. Hare wrote in his book *Cities of Southern Italy and Sicily*, "The principal curiosity of Taranto is the Mar Piccolo (about six miles long and three miles broad), with its active industries of fisheries and the propagation of fish . . . . The mode of farming mussels is that which was in existence in the twelfth century. Ropes are plunged into the water, and, when festooned with shells, are drawn up, and carried to the market, where the purchaser chooses his mussels himself, makes his bargain, and then has them detached."

The Mar Piccolo continued as a fishing preserve—for numerous species of fish as well as mussels and oysters—until 1889. In that year, the Italian government decided to locate the Royal Arsenal in Mar Piccolo, thus changing the character of the natural habitat.

Today, aquaculture and commercial fishing in Mar Piccolo are subject to the combined pressures of urbanization, industrialization and agriculture. From the surrounding urban communities including Taranto, fourteen pipes discharge sewage into Mar

Piccolo. The shipyard of the Italian Navy, including its dry docks, is located in the Primo Seno. Chemicals used by farmers in their fields outside Taranto leach into the water table or are carried as runoff into the rivers that feed into the Mar Piccolo.

Mussels are very sensitive to the water that surrounds them. Filter feeders, they quickly register any contaminants in their environment in their own flesh. For that reason, they are considered bio-indicators. Since the early 1900s, they have been the focus of many studies in the Mar Piccolo. Scientists can tell the health of the ecosystem by studying the health of the mussels living there.

The largest concentration of mussel farms in Italy using the "fixed" culturing system is located in the Gulf of Taranto, Puglia. Other traditional mussel-producing coastal and lagoon regions include La Spezia in Liguria, the Venetian Lagoon and the Flegreen Coast in Campania. More recent additions include the Friuli-Venezia Guilia coastal area of Trieste, the Gulf of Olbia in Sardegna, Emilia-Romagna and the Adriatic coast of Puglia. In addition to the "fixed" culturing system, *monoventia* (single long line) and Trieste *multiventia* (multiple long lines) systems are used.

The most recent development in mussel farming has been off-shore technologies that allow mussels to be grown outside lagoons and coastal areas—avoiding many environmental, health and hygiene problems. Off-shore mussels are grown using a suspension culture technique, evolved from the lagoon technique, that employs a floating structure, either on the surface or submerged, from which ropes are suspended. Off-shore production is carried out in Taranto, Mattinata, the Gulf of Trieste and the Gulf of Manfredonia.

The extensive commercial production of mussels has made them easily available. Creative cooks have devised many ways to serve them. Versatile, mussels can be steamed, fried, baked, or grilled, served plain or in a sauce. Every way, they are delicious.

In Puglia's provinces of Brindisi, Lecce and Taranto, a familiar dish is *Cozze alla Maniera Salentina*. Here is one way to prepare it:

Cozze alla Maniera Salentina

12 ounces or 300 grams of live mussels (these must be allowed to purge by soaking them for 24 hours in heavily salted water in the refrigerator)

- 1 pound or 500 grams of peeled, sliced potatoes
- 1 sliced white onion
- 1 small bunch minced parsley
- 2 tablespoons breadcrumbs
- 2 tablespoons grated pecorino cheese
- 2 beaten eggs
- Olive oil
- Sea salt and freshly ground pepper to taste

Scrub the mussels and pry them open over a bowl, saving the water from the shells. Put the mussels in a separate bowl and discard the shells.

In a pan that can be used in the oven, cook the sliced potatoes, onion and half the parsley in the water from the mussels and a little olive oil. Remove all but a thin layer of potato slices and place a thin layer of mussels on top of it. Dust the mussel layer with breadcrumbs, cheese and minced parsley. Follow with a second layer of potatoes, mussels, breadcrumbs, cheese and parsley. Pour the beaten egg over the top. Bake in a hot oven at 440° F or 220° C until the upper surface is crisp and golden.

If there is not enough time to prepare the dish above— or preferably visit Puglia itself—*Spaghetti alle Cozze* is a tasty alternative:

SPAGHETTI ALLE COZZE

Scrub the mussels and pry them open over a bowl, saving the water from the shells. Put the mussels in a separate bowl.

Heat olive oil with garlic slivers in a large pan, add fresh ground pepper and the mussels with a little of their own water. Add drained spaghetti, cooked very al dente, to the pan with the mussels. Add the rest of the mussel water and some of the water used to cook the pasta, if necessary. Continue cooking until pasta is ready to serve. Sprinkle with chopped parsley and more fresh ground pepper. *Delizioso!*

THE SASSI DI MATERA

DOREEN WOOD

n Matera, the *sassi* dwellers kept their chickens under the bed in their cave homes because there was nowhere else to keep them. Had they let them run outside, they'd likely have been stolen. Early in my life, I, too, spent time under the bed, also for safety reasons. Visiting a preserved typical *sassi*, I viewed the one large bed, rickety table, primitive implements and a model horse in its alcove. The curator described the crowding and smells: an average family of six children and four animals lived in one cavern. I called my own childhood impoverished until I saw the *sassi*. My early life circumstances were indeed tough, but not nearly equal to these harsh conditions. Even though these days I'm more fortunate, scenes of poverty still trigger memories.

The *sassi di Matera* (stones of Matera) resemble a jagged grey moonscape. The streets in some parts are located on rooftops. This ancient town grew on the slopes of several *gravine* (ravines). Named a UNESCO World Heritage Site in 1993, the dwellings developed from a prehistoric settlement and are believed to be some of the first human settlements in Italy. Over thousands of years, multiple generations of families lived in them. Located in Basilicata, sometimes referred to as Lucania, they are just over the border from Puglia. It's a strangely isolated region, cut off from the rest of Italy.

In 1935, Carlo Levi, an Italian painter trained as a doctor, arrived in Matera to spend a year as a political exile, banished for his anti-fascist writings by Mussolini. His classic book, *Christ Stopped at Eboli*, published in 1946, poetically describes the *sassi's* alien world of poverty and quiet despair. Director Francesco Rossi won many awards for his 1979 film adaptation of Levi's book. The similarity in the look of the *sassi* with that of the ancient sites in and around Jerusalem caught the eye of director Mel Gibson who used the site for his film *The Passion of the Christ*.

Levi's book is a series of poignant sketches. He describes the lives of peasants so grim, so impoverished, so imbued with what he called superstition and pagan ritual that he calls them "lost in time." *Christ Stopped in Eboli* is not about a deity that alighted in a place called Eboli, but rather about a region so remote and wild that civilization and, in Levi's perspective even Christ Himself, never got there. The *sassi* at Matera, which Levi reached by car, was the end of the road.

Levi said of the caves: "Inside those black holes, with earthen walls, I saw the beds, the poor furnishings, the rag spreads. On the floors were sprawled dogs, sheep, goats, and pigs. Each family had, in general, a single one of these caves for its entire residence and they all slept here together, men, women, children and animals. Twenty thousand people lived in this manner." When he arrived at Matera, the mayor told Levi not to associate with the peasants. The indolent gentry, professing Catholicism and enforcing its practices upon the villagers, governed neglectfully. But Levi was profoundly affected by the peasants' simple wisdom and their pagan rituals. He began to know and love the peasants. They began to call on him for medical emergencies, even though the local officials disapproved. The villagers formed a deep respect for this doctor who tended to them so compassionately; he in turn discovered the humanity and caring within their culture. Levi writes of tending to a dying peasant man and how sad and humiliated he was by the presence of death. He speaks of a great feeling of peace that pervaded his senses and the feeling that he had penetrated the very heart of the universe.

Ancient hydraulic aqueduct systems provided plenty of cool water to the *sassi*, but basic hygiene was almost non-existent. There was no sewage system in the *sassi*. Residents threw their slops and wastes into the stream in *la gravina* (the ravine). Mosquitoes and flies swarmed everywhere. Infections were rampant and the threat of the relentless, recurrent chills and fevers of malaria was ever present.

Until the middle of the twentieth century, women persevered in these suffocating windowless caverns with no electricity, refrigeration, plumbing or ventilation. There were few public outhouses. Men toiled in the nearby farms. Often the men left to emigrate to America or to serve in a war.

Levi observed that in every single dwelling two pictures hung: a print of President Franklin D. Roosevelt, a distant vision for betterment, "sort of an all-powerful Zeus;" the other was the Madonna of Viggiano, a black scowling face "appearing to be a pitiless, mysterious, ancient earth goddess." These cheap prints seemed to be the two faces of the powers that divide the universe between them.

In 1952, moved by Carlo Levi's book, the Italian government forcibly evicted fifteen thousand of the villagers from their *sassi*. They were moved into new apartment blocks, but their community was shattered.

Seeing the *sassi* reminded me of when I was a young girl during the late 1940s and early 1950s, when I lived with my family in a little dark green house in Winnipeg, Canada. Its crowded five rooms added up to about the size of a double car garage. Coming through the front door, the main room held a fraying maroon couch and three baby cribs. When tempers exploded in that confined space, I slid under a bed for safety. Unlike the animals in *sassi*, I read the funnies upside down until it was safe to come out.

A cylindrical oil-burning stove that dominated one wall

heated our tiny house for eight months of the year; its tortuous metal pipes curled up through the ceiling, sometimes overheating to a fiery dark red. Four children slept in a side room in steel bunk beds my father built. There would be two more babies born later. I remember trying to clean up a corner of the back room shed, desperately trying to create my own orderly space. My mother, father and nine children co-existed in that tiny space, living, eating, sleeping, fighting and playing. As was true for many of the *sassi* families, my father was periodically absent, working itinerant jobs. My mother, often swollen with a new pregnancy, worked relentlessly to feed us with meager resources. She scrubbed, toiled with her wringer-washer in the back shed, and hung bedding and diapers out to freeze into stiff sheets on the backyard line. We were desperately poor, but my mother persevered, a proud and often insouciant woman. But the *sassi* resemblance ends there. We had basic food while *sassi* inhabitants often went hungry. We had windows, electricity, refrigeration, plumbing and heat, whereas *sassi* inhabitants had none.

During his exile, Levi hired Giulia, a clean and conscientious village woman, as his housekeeper. She had lived in the same house for years with the priest, who had died. Even though large Roman Catholic churches and their outward trappings surrounded her, she was steeped in witchcraft and a belief in animal spirits. Levi said of Giulia, "She was forty-one years old, and she had had, between normal births and abortions, seventeen pregnancies by fifteen different men . . . . Almost all of her brood had died young. I never saw but one of them." As disparate as they were, the urbane intellectual and the pagan woman came to respect, care for and love each other.

Sassi village women had their own community. Matriarchal, they bonded together to enforce the basic rules of living and behavior. They reigned like queen bees over a mass of children, many of them illegitimate, which was not thought of as unusual. The priests often fathered many children with different women.

I imagined the life of a *sassi* mother. I envision Maria, probably one of thousands of Marias in the pagan-Catholic area. She had five children and another on the way. Early on that particular day her husband led their horse out of its alcove in the cave dwelling to go to works in the surrounding fields.

Her youngest baby slept in a basket hanging on the side of the bed, the others in rickety cots hanging on tenuous hooks. I envision her shooing two of the children outside, sweeping the earthen floors and with the most basic of cooking implements beginning to simmer their daily meal in the blackened iron pot hanging above a grate of flaming sticks in the cave's alcove.

On this day, two of her children lay listless on their tattered covers, shivering with chills and burning with fever. With her dark brows drawn together, Maria bathed them with cool water, placed amulets on their foreheads and muttered healing incantations. By the next week one of her children would be dead.

My mother, too, lost a baby in a raging red measles outbreak. I remember her howling at her loss.

The young proved that spirit survives despair. *Sassi* children were often thin, pale and listless, their bellies swollen from starvation. They sat in their doorways staring out at their limited world, or followed Levi down pathways begging for quinine to treat their malaria. Still, they harbored the playfulness of childhood. With only animals for company, their play seemed a mixture of young animal spirits. On simple carved wooden whistles, they played tunes that were often lively and cheerful.

As children in Winnipeg we played, too: howling cowboy and Indian races, tree climbing expeditions and turf fights with neighbors. Time and again one of us was confined to our little house with an illness. One of my sisters was kept in bed eight weeks with rheumatic fever; another sister was permanently scarred when, toddling around in her scooter in that tiny space, she inadvertently pulled a pot of boiling water on top of her small body. I, almost blind, broke my glasses periodically and had to stay in the house until my parents could afford to pay for another pair. I withdrew into an imaginary world of books where a fairy godmother would rescue me. Yes, the *sassi* community triggered memories, evoking feelings of isolation and despair.

In Matera, Levi found that true beauty and meaning in life did exist. He discovered that human values are stronger than the political values of the state. Although I left Winnipeg years ago, the bonds of love and family transcended poverty in my life as well.

THE ITALIAN MASSEUSE

LINDA WATANABE MCFERRIN

*T*he woman's hands were huge.

Or so it seemed as I lay in my skimpy paper underpants, standard issue at the thermal spa center in Santa Cesarea Terme, a tiny town on the coast of the Adriatic Sea in southern Puglia, at the absolute tip of the high heel of the boot that is Italy. She was a bit of a dominatrix, my masseuse, and I liked this about her: the way she slapped me around. Sometimes one needs a good dressing down.

I was at the tail-end of a lengthy stay in Europe that had included living the high life with jet-setting pals (one actually used the phrase "economy class scum" albeit ironically, to describe a certain tribe of travelers to which I did not immediately claim membership) in London. I'd been wined and dined at glamorous private cocktail parties and escorted about the city to plays, restaurants and museums—all of this with a big black cast on my injured left wrist and hand—and though I was hanging out with a first-class crowd, I will confess here that I am, at heart, economy class scum, which means that I'll do what I need to do to get a ticket to ride, including sitting, knees pressed to chest, in the cheapest seats in the house. I would do the same for any of Shakespeare's plays, which I approach with similar jubilation and enthusiasm. I'd stand for heaven's sake. And I would stand on a plane, too, if it meant my flight dollars went further. I am actually one of those people *designed* with economy class in mind. I am five foot one and 435/455ths of an inch in height—unless I am wearing stiletto heels, which I almost never do—and I weigh, well . . . let's just say I weigh less than one of the larger breeds of dogs.

When I sit in first class—which I've had the honor and discomfort of doing from time to time—I cannot bend my legs, as the edge of the large seat is closer to my ankles than my knees and my feet stick straight out . . . unless I wiggle forward in the seat and fill the open area between my spine and the seat back with huge numbers of those tiny, made-for-an-airplane-snooze pillows. Either way it's an unpleasant ride and I've often thought of auctioning my seat off to some super-sized person miserably crammed into economy class accommodations.

I realize this is quite a preamble. All of this is simply to supply you with a little background information. I just want you to understand my state of mind as I lay there naked, but for those paper undies, at the mercy of my masseuse's ham-sized mitts. I must admit I was worried. She was very rough and I am, even in my relative youth, quite decrepit.

Take that black cast for example: I'd broken my hand right before I left for Europe when I was attacked by a pit bull in Stockton, California, and forced to the ground. What was even more aggravating was that I'd had the area cast only a few years before when I shattered my wrist in Holland whilst on a bike on the dyke that circles the Isselmeer. What I like to call my bionic wrist, because of all of the metal in it, was having an unpleasant soft-tissue flashback due to the new injury. That was keeping me up nights and the black cast was cramping my style, both kinetically and cosmetically, though friends had assured me that they had mistaken it for a quirky and delightfully Goth fashion accessory. Have you ever heard of a bracelet that keeps you from taking a shower or limits the number of pieces of luggage (must-have camera, laptop, backpack, needlessly large pairs of shoes for various sports, clothes, heavy recreational reading) that you can comfortably carry?

I should reveal, as long as I'm on the subject and the masseuse still hovers above me, that I also have metal parts in my leg due to what I cavalierly claim was a fall from a barstool around one year ago. The injury is not yet completely healed. No matter, I still get around . . . so the high life continued in Italy: in Rome and in Puglia where we criss-crossed the length and breadth of the region while the feasts rolled past with clockwork precision and I, who am allergic to gluten, shellfish and caffeine and generally averse to the consumption of red meat, was finding it hard to keep these fine but afflictive substances out of my ridiculously finicky system. So by the time the masseuse had me, I was exhibiting celiac-like symptoms: swollen throat, elbows broken out in a rash and an unpleasant feeling of bloat, in spite of what I felt was an assiduous attention to what went into my mouth and what came out of it (after all, it was a gathering of very clever writers).

So you see, not to whine, but I really needed the massage and a good dressing down, a contemplative slap on the buttocks as if to say, "Hey, aren't you getting a little ahead of yourself? Shouldn't you slow down and smell, rather than drink, all that coffee?"

And what better place to do this than on the massage tables of a therapeutic facility known far and wide for the treatment of various physical, rheumatological, cardiological, dermatological, gynecological and rhynogeneous complaints? The place is a veritable clinic by the sea. It has that air of relapse and recovery for which, I'm sure, the great spas of the world were once celebrated—that is before spas became more cosmetic than curative. It even smelled deeply reparative, with its sulfur pools, mineral muds and the faint but pervasive odor of perspiration that mingled ever so subtly with the cleaner chemical notes.

The name of my masseuse was Celestina, I believe—a particularly good name for a woman with the hands to heal. Celestina covered me in mud, let me wallow in it for a while then threw me into a tub for a pummeling hydro-massage. I was nearly comatose by the time she retrieved me and ushered me into the quiet room where she planned to attack my every ache and pain. That's when she presented me with the undies and arranged me face down on her table.

"*Si chiamo che?*" I had slurred incorrectly and indecipherably into the sheet as she vigorously assaulted my thighs. Did I mention that her massage table, like all of those at this facility, I imagine, did not have a hole for your face to poke through and that my neck had to twist in an ungodly fashion (old movie buffs, I am referring to *The Exorcist*)—a posture that I found hard to achieve—in order to be understood?

"Celestina," she said. "*Come si chiama lei?*"

"*Mio Linda,*" I mangled, drooling into table and sheet, not the least bit embarrassed by the primitive manner whereby I was communicating. I was in paper underpants, wasn't I?

"Lin?" she responded.

"No, Linda," I slurped. "Ohhhh, that feels great."

"*Eh . . . piacere di conoscerla. Parla italiano, lei?*" she inquired.

"No. *Non parlo.* But I'm trying," I slobbered.

Our conversation proceeded in a sloppy, halting way and I learned that Celestina had lived her entire life in the province of Lecce, in Salento, the southernmost portion of Puglia and that she did not speak French or Spanish or English or Japanese, none of which I can speak effectively either, though I sometimes pretend to. At least I *think* that's what she said. I also think she told me that she had three children; that one son was a musician, one a garbage man or a member of the Mafia—I'm not sure which—and that her third and youngest child, a girl, was mentally impaired and living in an institution.

"*Oh, che tristessa.* (Oh, what sadness!)" I said, commiserating and feeling an immediate bond.

"*Si,*" she responded punching me in the way that a good Italian chef will punch the air out of pizza dough.

"*Anche mio.* (Me too)," I confessed and explained to her, in the slack-jawed pastiche of sounds that I have come to call pidgin spitalian, that my daughter, Marissa, had died shortly after she was born and that I have never gotten over it.

She was silent. The room filled with the sound of her breathing and mine. Then a small droplet bounced onto the bare skin between my shoulder blades. She wiped it away and her large, warm hands sank deeply into the trapezoid of muscle stretched tightly between my clavicles. "The world is sad," I think she said.

Celestina was extremely attentive. When she came to my right ankle with its symmetrical scars, she asked tenderly, "*Cosa è successo?*"

"Mucho injury," I responded, switching for some reason to Spanglish as she proceeded to unknot those tendons.

What happened after that? She flipped me like a pancake and covered me in an oily substance, telling me my skin was "*magnifico.*"

"Shank you," I drooled, by now totally punch-drunk and stupid. It was hard getting dressed. I could barely button my shirt. I staggered out into the brilliant sunlight and sat, wrapped in a long-sleeved white shirt, hatted and sunglassed, as covered as I had moments before been exposed. Nancy, one of the writers, drifted by and we took a stroll together, finding a room filled with machines for the thermal treatment of ear and nose related diseases: adenoid hypertrophy, chronic pharyngitis, recurring pharynx-tonsillitis, allergy rhinitis, nasal polyposis, rhine-bronchial syndrome, chronic sinusitis, various forms of catarrh and much, much more. In the spa's inhalations treatment department, row upon row of flowing water contraptions, each with an empty chair in front of it, stood ready to bath the noses and throats of the afflicted. Of course neither Nancy nor I could fathom what the machines were for, though the various knobs and dials and the yellowing plastic tubes and masks suggested snot, mucus and sulfurous solutions—a combination quite unappealing on every possible level. We left shaking our heads.

Back outside, I took a seat again on the terrace, looking out over the sulfur pool and the Grottos Gattulia, Solfurea and Fetida, across the turquoise waters of the Adriatic toward that exquisite point where the sea meets the sky. There I waited in a peeled and polished kind of oblivion, like a patient in a chamber before a transfer, feeling old but transformed, turned inside out and ready for whatever was to come, totally intoxicated by the sense of physical ruin and spiritual repair. The other writers gathered and lounged, looking nearly as bleary as I. I wondered what miracles they had found in their separate rooms, what doors to the soul had been unlocked, what demons routed.

It was late when we left, the ride home long and debilitating in the gentlest of ways. The next day I would find bruises all over my thighs and sigh. Of course the sojourn in Puglia was not over; it would go on, as life tends to go on and on and on. But I would remember Celestina, I thought, and the ministrations of Santa Cesarea Terme, and the way the sea on that strip of coast in Salento slapped at the rock hard until it formed beautiful coves and grottos. And I would remember those soft, hard, kind, brutal hands, and I would be left with longing.

LETTER TO ISABELLA

SANDRA BRACKEN

June 2008, Puglia

*D*ear Isabella,

As the bus passes the turn for Corato, I think of you. I had no idea I would be so close to your home town. If you were sitting next to me, as you were the day we met on the train, we'd probably talk about *agriturismo* and lunch at Tenuta Pedale. You can imagine my curiosity about the fortified farms called *masserie*. Today, as a hotel, Tenuta Pedale serves produce grown on the land that surrounds it, including its own wine. It dates from 1600 and the food is *biologica*, organic. The meal, served family style, gave us many dishes to choose from during each course. I still taste the perfectly ripe sweet cherries set out in big white bowls on the long table, just when I thought our meal was over. The meals in Puglia are feasts: I think of the antipasti, then the *primi, secondi, contorni* and *dolci*. Our tours are sandwiched between meals. It is difficult to say which dish, which *ristorante* or *masseria* is my favorite. The *cozze terra d' Otranto* (mussels) at Ristorante Orsa Maggiore are tiny, tender and sweet. I can make a meal of the octopus salad at L'Ancora Sul Mare, perfectly seasoned with the salty taste of the sea, lemon juice and olive oil. I find myself enjoying the antipasti so much that I have too little room for the pasta course, let alone the *secondo*. The *parmigiana melanzone* (eggplant) as it is prepared at La Sommita is so delicate the flavors melt together—a memorable moment. I find it interesting that the fava bean dish, cooked with chicory and mashed, is served as an antipasto: then when the consistency is slightly changed it becomes a sauce for *fricielli* (pasta) at Ristorante Casa Nova.

My introduction to these new combinations of ingredients is certainly expanding my cooking ideas. These are dishes whose focus is simplicity, using what is local and fresh. This is what I like in my own cooking. I am encouraged to be more inventive—use more olives, perhaps. However, I know that even if I use the same components, the end result will not taste the same. I cannot recreate the intensity of flavors that comes from Puglia's farms, or from the sea that surrounds your peninsula. This culinary journey far surpasses your introduction on the the train.

I can hear you saying "you must try *burrata*," the fresh mozzarella with a creamy interior, unique to the south. I agree,

Isabella, it is distinct and tasty, but truthfully, I enjoy the various forms of ricotta more. Sadly there are too many cheeses I want to try—the *scamorza di pecora* from Corato for example. But there is just too little time.

Also, as you suggested, I sample as many of the local wines as I am able to, there are so many! At the Azienda Agricola Conte Spagnolletti Zeuli, we have the opportunity to taste both wine and olive oil. I buy both, drink the wine, but won't open the extra-virgin olive oil until I am home. Their Terranera DOC *riserva* is very much to my liking—straightforward and robust.

When I told you that I intended to walk as much as possible, you suggested I put the map aside. I am taking your advice. You must have known that the many country lanes surrounding Alberobello always intersect no matter which way I turn. There is one hill high enough where looking west, I can see all the way to Putignano. Closer to town I come to a rise where another view opens up. The road slopes to a narrow valley shining in the early morning sunlight, a fresh green patchwork of fields, bordered with trees. There is an occasional *trullo*. I could be in a fairy tale. But as you know, this is a very real scene with people who work hard to keep the land productive. It seems incredible to me and indicates labor and dedication that so much is grown in soil that is a shallow layer over solid limestone. It makes sense that fields and properties are enclosed by stone walls. There is such variety I never tire of the discoveries. Most of the larger fields are filled with olive trees. On the periphery, almonds, walnuts, hazelnuts, plums, cherries, pears, loquat and figs are some other trees that I recognize. Then row after row the ubiquitous grapes grow next to plots of vegetables—artichokes, zucchini, peas, beans, tomatoes, peppers and *cocameri* (fat cucumbers, crispy and mild).

Where one stone wall ends, another begins, giving all the wildflowers at the edge of the road a stunning backdrop. What daily pleasure to come upon mile after mile of color. I do not make much progress, wanting to stop to enjoy them—poppies, cranesbill, scabiosa, mullein, golden star and other yellow wild-flowers whose names I confuse. The occasional snapdragons, bergenia and larkspur have probably escaped from a domestic garden.

Did you know that Queen Anne's lace and chicory are plants you see in great abundance in rural Virginia where I spent my childhood? I am not surprised to find the herbs rosemary, laven-der and santolina. I like learning about new plants: this time it is *cappero*, the caper plant. The blossom is beautiful, creamy white petals with feathery purple stamen. It seems to grow in the most unlikely places. I saw one bush hanging between stones on a wall. I picked some of the buds to see if I could detect the distinctive aroma. It's there, but I understand the flavor increases as it dries.

Every morning I am passed by an older man on a motor scooter in helmet and wool suit jacket over well-worn trousers. Finally, one day I see him kneeling in one of the smaller garden plots picking zucchini. We say *buongiorno* simultaneously. It is nice to see his face, the earnest face of the person who cares for this neat, well-kept garden. His peas are coming along nicely and there are many blossoms on his tomatoes.

Isabella, do you remember that you sent me on a search for a particular variety of figs? I found it! The larger fig is just now ripe and the second crop is visible as a small bud on the same tree. The one I tasted was warm, soft and fully-flavored. Remembering this delight, I will look after my little tree in Maryland with greater care and anticipation.

I criss-cross the peninsula of Puglia with the writers in the workshop, gathering a brief history. We enjoy an evening *passeggiata* (stroll) in Martina Franca and Lecce admiring the intricately carved stonework on the baroque buildings.

You thought I would be impressed by the lovely white cities of Ostuni and Oria. I am. From the hill of Castel del Monte, I look across the flat plain in all directions hoping to catch a glimpse of both the Adriatic and Ionian Seas.

I often wonder who will open the next door. As it turns out, after our lunch at Tenute Al Bano Carrisi, the man himself personally takes the afternoon to show us around his *masseria*. He may be a popular singer, but I'll remember most his warmth and generosity and his thoughts on Puglia. He, like you, Isabella, wears his pride on his sleeve. Both of you have traveled the world and continue to return home to Puglia, not so much out of habit but because of your deep affection and understanding of this place. You are devoted to the people and the way of life here: you know how complete it is.

Isabella, *sono cosi fortunato ad averti incontrato.* (I am so lucky to have met you.) *Grazie mille* for giving me the best introduction to Puglia I can imagine; for coloring my experience with passion and sensitivity. I see your heart on the *cartina* you created for me on the train. It now has my own affectionate smears—and notes for another time.

Twirling for Lepers

Denise Altobello

"*I* used to twirl for lepers," I confided to Joanna and Roger. Roger stared at me and asked, "Really? New Orleans has a leper colony?"

"Actually, no. The colony was a bit upriver from New Orleans," I clarified, "but just before Mardi Gras, we majorettes used to take our batons to Carville to entertain the lepers with a parade. Twirling was our ministry."

Standing in front of the statue of Santo Damiano—physician to the poor, servant to outcasts and oddly enough, patron saint of lepers—in the Basilica Cattedrale of Maria Assunto in Brindisi's diocese of Oria, I felt the unexpected but familiar pulse of south Louisiana's dark and quirky history deep in the heart of sunny Puglia.

Puglia and New Orleans are both southern regions of aching

beauty and plenty. Sure, some of that *plenty* comes in the way of hardships: hot summers, sluggish economies, weak infrastructure and continuous allegations of corrupt government. But like many in my city across the sea, the Pugliesi that I met proudly suffer such indignities for the pleasure of living in a culture that meets both the worst of times and the best of times with the support of family, food and ritual—not to mention a healthy shot of defiant good humor.

Just as Huey Long promised Depression-era Louisianians, "Every man a king," and "a chicken in every pot," proud Pugliesi providers found an imaginative way to assure that meat appeared on every dinner plate even during the leanest times. Scarce communal meals rested upon platters painted with the *galluzzo*, a little rooster hiding beneath the pasta. Today, dishes, platters, cups and jugs from the ceramic factories of Grottaglie are prized for their rooster trademark. Making the best of hardship often requires making a joke of it, and the jovial Pugliesi I met were certainly adept at doing so.

One Sunday morning in Alberobello's Bar al Corso, I chatted with Cesare, the cappuccino-maestro, about how similar Puglian traditions are to some in New Orleans. He summed up his explanation for this in two words: *povero e cattolico*. With this shared membership in the society of poor Catholics established, I asked, "*Cesare, conoscete Santo Damiano?*"

"*Si, abbiamo una grande festival per lui in settembre. Ci è una parata, una massa e musica sul viale.*" Interesting. They have a great festival with a mass, a parade and music in the streets.

"*Una parata? Fantastico!*" A parade? Sounds like home to me—only without majorettes, I suppose. Days later, my research uncovered more details about the festival. Unfortunately, the research also disclosed that my Saint Damien—friend to lepers— was simply a fan and, therefore, namesake of the Alberobello patron. Darn! Nevertheless, Puglia's icon is honored annually in a style befitting a Louisiana legend. A twenty-four hour mass, live brass bands, street performers and a grand fireworks exhibition precede the parade where his statue is carried to the *Piazza del Popolo*, the Piazza of the People. Excited, I told Cesare about the Italian-American Society's Saint Joseph's Day parade in New Orleans each year that showcases bands and flower-bedecked floats. I popped open my laptop and proudly pointed to photos of my Italian husband marching with his brother, cousins and uncle in tuxedoes set off by green, white and red cummerbunds.

Amazed when he heard that the parade concludes with a ball where everyone sips wine and dances the *tarantella*, he repeated,

"*La tarantella?*"

"*Si!*"

"*Come Alberobello, no?*" Alberobello's frantic version was allegedly popularized by crazed tarantula victims in the nearby city of Taranto.

"*No, come Napoli!* Like the wedding dance in *The Godfather.*

"*Ah, si,*" Cesare sighed in disappointment.

Intrigued about these Italian influences in New Orleans, a

dark-suited older gentleman named Antonio looked up from reading his *Gazatta Sportiva* at the bar. In English that was mercifully better than my Italian, he asked about my interest in Santo Damiano, patron of Alberobello. Both he and Cesare laughed as I used a knife to pantomime my baton twirling for Padre Damiano's *lepers* in Louisiana. Fortunately for all of us, it turns out that leper in Italian is the same as in English.

Spurred on by their "*Bravos*," I described Saint Joseph altars that Italians in my city painstakingly prepare for weeks leading up to the patron's feast day on March 19. I explained that the food-laden altars are often erected in homes of families of only moderate means to thank Saint Joseph for the blessings of the year. I described altars set with pictures of Saint Joseph tucked among heaping platters of lasagna, spaghetti with anchovies, aromatic fennel bulbs as well as endless trays of anise and sesame cakes punctuating the feast. Abundant offerings ward off future deprivation. Miraculously, Antonio understood my Tarzan Italian and nodded his head in approval of my story. "*Eh*," he said, "*come in Puglia, mangiamo e ricodiamo.*" He kissed his fingertips and brought them to his heart. "Eat and remember." The anthem of both of our food cultures.

A question about another New Orleans tradition popped into my head. "Antonio, *il fava—è buona fortuna?* I wondered whether the dried fava—"lucky bean"—that we prayerfully stash in the private recesses of our pocketbooks for future security is revered in Puglia. Cesare moved in on the action here. He motioned

Antonio to be silent and answered with authority,

"*Il fava? No, ma abbiamo la melagrana per buona fortuna.*"

A big melon for luck? Confounded, I offered Cesare my pen and one of his own napkins to draw the mysterious *melagrana*. After three attempts, he darted behind the bar and pointed to a picture of Jesus. Lo and behold, the Jesus lurking beside the *grappa* had neither a shepherd's staff nor a burning heart. But he did have a gentle smile and what appeared to be a pomegranate in his open hand.

"Pomegranate!" I exclaimed.

"*Sì*", Cesare smiled, "pomegranate." The fruit of promise in times of despair. Kind of like Padre Damiano. Kind of like the lucky bean. And kind of like the rooster staring up from the communal plate.

My days in sunny Puglia moved along. Again and again, the juxtaposition of hardship and humor tugged the chords of remembrance. In Grottaglie, where the rooster is king, I came face to face—actually, breast to breast—with a *pupa con baffo*, a much sought-after moustached doll that is a feudal version of traditional New Orleans defiance and comic lewdness.

"These would look quite at home among my Mardi Gras decorations," I murmured. "If only the captain of the Krewe of Satyricon could have a look at these big bosomed, cross-dressing, bearded guardians of maidenhood and maidenheads. The *pupa* may inspire the theme for next year's carnival ball."

Francesco, another silver-haired Pugliese, pressed an opened Nicola Fasano ceramic catalog into my hand. He pointed to a page devoted to nine versions of the ceramic *pupe*—some *con i baffi* (with moustaches), others without. Some stood tall beside the hearth. Others sported cylindrical tubes ready for conversion to buxom table lamps. Francesco drew my attention to the English translation of Puglia's proud legend of a jealous husband-to-be determined to escape the unacceptable dishonor of having his bride deflowered by the lord of the estate. So the hapless groom disguised himself as a woman to trick the rapacious liege. The trick did not succeed though because the eager young groom forgot to shave his moustache. Hmm . . . .

Now there's a story that would raise the collective eyebrow of many a Mardi Gras cross-dresser. I smiled again at our shared capacity to paint over misfortune and injustice with the brush of broad and bawdy humor.

I remembered the amazement of many Americans when New Orleans celebrated Mardi Gras just six months after Lady Katrina blew through her levees and deflowered her coast. Despite the fact that so many residents were still living in either evacuation cities, dark government-issued trailers or under blue tarp roofs, the wounded city embraced its collective misery and still radiated with music, parades and hilarity for the abbreviated Carnival season. The satirical Krewe de Vieux, unique because it still relies on hand or mule-drawn floats to poke fun at local wretchedness kicked off the merry mayhem when it rolled through the French

Quarter on February 11, 2006. What a six months it had been! So, what was the Krewe's theme for 2006? *C'est Levee! Life's a breach.*

"Yep," I mused, "the Pugliesi would understand. Like a majorette before lepers, the breasts on the *pupa* lamp base swelled proudly in approval.

COULD I EAT A HORSE?

LAURIE McANDISH KING

*T*he instructions were unnerving: *Boil olive oil in a hot pan, lay the horsemeat in flat, and turn it when it starts to rise.* I tried hard not to visualize horseflesh rearing up out of a pan of boiling oil.

We were in search of the "Puglian delicacy" I had read about in a guidebook and was determined not to miss. My plan was to find a restaurant that served horsemeat, convince one of my more adventuresome traveling companions to order it, and then to beg the smallest bite, just a tiny taste—after all, it was a regional specialty. But things did not work out according to my plan.

I first asked at Casa Nova in Alberobello. It was a white-tablecloth restaurant with a large menu, and seemed a likely source. But I was met with a puzzled expression. No, they did not serve *carne de cavalle*.

Perhaps the waiter did not understand my broken Italian. "Horse, *cavalle?*" I repeated, pantomiming a gallop. I felt foolish pantomiming in a nice restaurant, but I was halfway around the world and really wanted to try horsemeat.

"No. No *cavalle*."

No matter; we still had more than a week to go. I would find it at the next restaurant. I persisted at Osteria degli Angeli in Lecci, at Ristorante Orsa Maggiore in Castro Marina and at La Sommita in Ostuni. Surely these fine Puglian establishments served the local specialty. But not a single one offered it. I tried requesting *carne equine*, thinking perhaps I had used the wrong word, but no matter how I asked, horsemeat was simply not on the menu. I enlisted the assistance of my travel companions: would they help me find a menu with horsemeat?

"Horsemeat?" M.J. asked incredulously. "You want to eat *horsemeat?* Why?"

"It's a specialty of the region," I explained.

"I thought you were a vegetarian. How could you eat Mr. Ed?"

"I'm not completely. And I just want to try him. I mean *it*."

They promised to help look. Days passed, but no one found *cavalle*. (If I had not been looking myself, I would have doubted their sincerity.) Taking a seat one evening at La Cantina, I had nearly given up the search, when Connie and Linda spotted *Involtino al sugo di vitello o puledro* on the menu and alerted me from across the room.

"Rolls of veal or horse and tomatoes," the translation read.

There it was.

In that moment, when I expected to feel delight, a seed of doubt arose. I was not certain whether I could actually eat an equine. I had never owned a horse; my personal experience of them was not unlike my experience of cows, seen chiefly in rural fields, and from a distance. I eat steak occasionally, but I began to worry that horses might somehow be different. Could I actually consume a Seabiscuit steak? A Black Beauty roast? Filet o' Flicka?

My companions were watching, waiting—probably thinking I would not go through with it. I ordered the *puledro*.

The waiter raised his eyebrow in what I took to be a disapproving look. Although horsemeat was listed on the menu, he informed me, La Cantina was not serving it tonight.

I began to wonder whether the dish really existed. Perhaps it was the Puglian equivalent of an urban legend, making for colorful copy in the guidebooks, teasing tourists, even appearing on the occasional menu, but never materializing in an actual meal. And perhaps that was just as well.

But Annelize assured me that horsemeat is indeed eaten in Europe. "It is common in France, where culinary appreciation surpasses sentimentality," she explained. This perspective momentarily renewed my resolve, as I am not accustomed to being accused of sentimentality.

"I ate it a lot as a student in Holland. It is very tender in comparison to the average beef," Annelize continued. "The muscle structure is somewhat coarser, the taste a little sweeter. I imagine it is comparable to human flesh; that is what cannibals report."

Cannibals? I did not like the direction this was heading!

The expression on my face must have matched my flagging enthusiasm, because later that evening Chrysa took it upon herself to assist in the quest. Since I had had no success at restaurants, we switched to butcher shops. If they served the restaurant business, they would be able to tell us which restaurants to try. We located a butcher shop that sold beef, veal, goat, sheep, pork, chicken . . . everything, it seemed, *except* horsemeat.

"*Si vendono il carne de cavalle?* Do you sell horsemeat?"

"*Cavalle?* No."

Did they know where we might find it?

"No."

We had better luck at a second butcher shop. Although they did not carry *cavalle*, they reluctantly sent us "down the hill, turn left, then turn right." We followed the directions, and ended up at a deli. No *cavalle*.

Chrysa persisted, searching up and down Alberobello's steep, narrow streets. Three hundred meters down the main road, Largo Martellotta, she saw the sign: Macelleria Carne Equina. (Surely the locals all knew it.) A second sign outside the shop featured a large horse's head.

Inside, Giovanni was sweeping up for the night. Not that there was anything to sweep; the store was spotless. All the meat had been put away for the evening. The empty glass cases and stainless steel counter sparkled. Gleaming white tile walls were sparsely decorated with framed photos of horses and donkeys. I was relieved that they had already closed.

"*Si vendono il carne de cavalle?*" Chrysa asked, poking her head through the open door.

"*Si.* Would you like some?" Giovanni pulled out a chunk of meat the size of . . . well, the size of a horse's head. It *wasn't* a head, of course. It was bright red and marbled with white, and it gave me the creeps. This was the real thing. He cut us two thin steaks.

At five euro and change for almost half a kilogram, our horse-meat cost less than twelve euro per kilo. Lamb, by way of comparison, was twenty euro per kilos in the butcher shop down the street; veal was twenty-two. Suddenly I understood why no one had wanted to serve me *cavalle*: it was *budget* food, most commonly eaten by students and others for whom price was a major consideration.

Giovanni showed us four pieces of paper, neatly stapled together. The first was a *Certificato Sanitario*, a health certificate pronouncing the meat *livero consumo*. (My best guess at a translation was "freed for eating." I don't think the horse's liver was being singled out.) The remaining three papers documented Giovanni's purchase of the horse that had supplied our steaks, the name and address of the seller, our horse's name and birthday, the name of the ranch where it grew up, its parents, their bloodline, the date and place of the slaughter . . . the horse's upbringing and education, for all I know.

My resolve weakened.

Giovanni's wife, Dina, explained how to prepare the steaks. "Boil olive oil in a hot pan, lay the horsemeat in flat, and turn it when it starts to rise."

"Then what?"

"*Sale*, salt." Realizing that we were tourists and probably did not have our own supply of seasonings, Dina was kind enough to put a little salt into a plastic bag and send it home with us. A pinch of salt after we cooked it was all the steak needed, she assured us.

Chrysa and I thanked Giovanni and Dina and left them to lock up the shop. We stopped at the deli to pick up a few other things for dinner, in case the horsemeat tasted awful. Back at our *trullo*, Chrysa fried the steaks according to Dina's instructions; they "rose" in the pan when cooked, just as she had said they would. I cut up fresh tomatoes and mozzarella. We rearranged some wildflowers M.J. had gathered on her morning run, played Chrysa's new *Al Bano Platinum* CD on my laptop computer, and set as pretty a table as we could. We wanted a pleasant ambience for our first taste.

Chrysa was braver than I; she tried it first.

She liked it.

I swallowed my tomato and had a gulp of water before slicing off a piece of meat. I wasn't going to eat it with anything else; I wanted to really taste the horse. The first bite was moist and tender. It was delicious!

It tasted just like beef.

ST. CHRYSANTHUS AT ORIA

CHRYSA TSAKOPOULOS

T came to Puglia anticipating verdant rolling hills laced with purple strands of grapevines and speckled with ancient olive groves bathed in golden light cascading from the heavens. Perhaps even a sumptuous meal of *orechiette* and *burrata* with a Giancarlo Giannini look-alike in a starlit piazza. But in the end, my greatest gift was bones.

My Puglian sojourn began in Rome. I navigated my way between tourists, carabinieri and gypsies to land in Alessandro's taxi.

"Tell me, what are you called?" the solemn, sapphire-eyed Alessandro inquired as his hand gently stroked the black leather steering wheel before him.

"Chrysa," I lazily replied.

"Chrystal, Christine?"

"No. Chrysa. It is short for *Crisantemo*, you know, the flower." The white taxi abruptly swerved, barely sparing the lives of innocent pedestrians strolling beside us.

"*Che? Non lo credo!* (What? I don't believe it!) Is not so nice name to have." Unlike in England, where chrysanthemums adorn weddings, in Italy they adorn coffins.

Alessandro gasped in his elementary English, overwhelmed by the revelation of my moniker. "*Non lo direi a nessuno* (I would not say this to anybody)," he warned. Luckily at that moment, we screeched to a halt in front of the hotel. I grabbed my suitcase from Alessandro and rushed inside.

A few days later, after I had settled in my *trullo* in Alberobello with fellow writers Laurie and Mary Jean, the group was scheduled to visit the white city of Oria. Our oversized bus lurched over the sun-drenched hills through the golden fields of Puglia. Scenic white and yellow houses were sprinkled across the countryside with the fuchsia and magenta vines of bougainvillea stretching their elegant fingers over the balconies. Crimson poppies lounged in the meadows of summer crops. Before us rose a statuesque hill with white houses pouring from its summit.

Oria keeps watch over the surrounding landscape from her home on a hill. The city glistens white covered in syrupy sunbeams as the top of the Basilica pierces the cloudless sky. My fellow writers and I ascended vertical paths of slippery stone that wove through the narrow streets of the town. I had no idea of my appointment with destiny.

In the vaulted medieval room where lunch was served, I began thumbing through the tourist guide of Oria. My fingers suddenly froze.

"My God they're here!" I exclaimed. Leaping off my chair over fellow writer Carol and ramming into the waiter's left shoulder, I proceeded to call the attention of the restaurant's entire clientele.

"Everybody, please listen! They're here. The bones of my saint, St. Chrysanthus, are in Oria!" I sputtered, spilling my wine all over myself and the poor chap at the table next to me. Alas, my guardian angel was either on vacation or laughing too hard to protect me, for I proceeded to propose an unintelligible toast in honor of my beloved St. Chrysanthus and his wife St. Daria to my bewildered yet obviously amused audience. Luckily for everyone, I finally returned to my table.

As a Greek Orthodox, I firmly believe in the power of my name saint to intercede on my behalf. A pilgrimage to visit the relics of one's name saint can be a life-changing event. Having believed for many years that St. Chrysanthus had been burned alive and that no relics therefore existed, I had long given up the hope for such a pilgrimage. All this had changed. I frantically turned to our ebullient and friendly guide that day.

"*Professore* Pino!" I pleaded, "Can we go and see the relics, *per favore?*"

"No, *cara* (dear) they are closed and won't be open until later this evening." Alas, it would be impossible to visit them that day.

It was only a small setback. Pilgrims survived journeys across fierce Mediterranean tempests and the hot and desiccated sands of Arabia on the way to spiritual enlightenment. I could brave the sinewy Puglian roads, armed with nothing but notebook and attitude to return to the Castello Svevo di Oria.

Back in Alberobello, I searched for someone willing to listen to my tale. I found Beppe, the young curator of the olive oil museum across from my *trullo*, who took great pleasure in correcting my Italian.

"Who?" Beppe asked me, his blue eyes glistening in the afternoon light.

"Saints Chrysanthus and Daria, two of the most important saints in Christendom." In my imperfect Italian, I proceeded to tell the story: Chrysanthus was the son of a wealthy pagan nobleman in Alexandria, Egypt. On a trip to Rome with his father Polemius, he was converted to Christianity. His father panicked, trying his utmost to make the young man apostatize. As a final effort, Polemius arranged for the marriage of Chrysanthus to Daria, a wealthy pagan woman from Athens, Greece. Hoping that her charm and learnedness would lure the young convert back to paganism, Polemius was disappointed, for the plan did not have the desired effects. Daria instead followed her husband into Christianity, and the couple was buried alive in a pit of mire.

"*Il viaggio di Crisante non è fermata là perchè l'ho trovato ad Oria!* (But Chrysanthus' journey did not stop there because I found him in Oria!)" In the early ninth century, Pope Stephan V gave the bones to Bishop Theodosius in order to build a cathedral. The saints became the first protectors of Oria, and there they remain. I was going to find them, I triumphantly concluded.

Beppe nodded, gave me a supportive look, and we parted ways.

The next morning, Laurie, who had graciously agreed to accompany me on my quest, and I hopped into the back of a hired car. The car sailed over the black roads, reaching our destination in half the time of our previous visit. Whizzing up the hill, we gazed on the tall towers of the castle stretching their necks to the heavens. Once a cathedral, Emperor Frederick II decided, upon marrying his second wife Yolanda in 1225, to convert the site into a fortress. My saint's bones lay safe in the palace's womb below.

Laurie and I were dropped off in a piazza not far from the castle grounds. After ten minutes of following the pointed fingers of locals, we arrived at the front office: closed. Noticing an open gate, Laurie and I wandered up a stone staircase where a locked iron gate greeted us.

"*Posso auitarvi?* (May I help you?)" an invisible voice questioned. Before I could answer, the voice's body appeared behind the gate.

"Where can we buy tickets?" I asked, reminding him that we were members of the writing group that had visited the day before.

"Oh, for you no problem. Just come in and take pictures."

I explained to the curator that we were interested in seeing the crypt of the Saints Chrysanthus and Daria.

"*La cripta è chiusa* (The crypt is closed)," he summarily informed me.

I tried to explain my special relationship to Saint Chrysanthus.

"*Ma Sainte Crisante è un'uomo* (But Saint Chrysanthus is a man)," he responded, visibly perplexed.

I told him I knew, but my name was the feminine version. My face melted in disappointment.

"Did you come all the way here to see the crypt?" he asked, relenting.

"Yes," I begged. He called to a colleague and grabbed some keys. In the dim light, Laurie and I followed him down cracked stone steps.

Behind a veil of insect webs, Laurie and I beheld three wall frescoes dating from the construction of the crypt, one of Saint Paul, one of Chrysanthus and one of Daria. Soft beams of white light filtered through holes in the ceiling. The curator began his speech on the origins of the structure, but I could not hear. Gazing at the timeworn painting, I started to sob uncontrollably.

Our guide turned around. "Why are you crying?"

I just shook my head. "Where are the bones?" I whispered.

The man informed me that they were in the Basilica, and that he would be glad to lead Laurie and me there.

The Basilica stood stoically facing west, its façade rose-colored, ornamented with coats of arms of the Bishop, the Pope and the city of Oria. Tall columns with painted marble veins spiraled up to the ceiling, and a great portrait of the Saints Cosimo and Damiano warmly greeted the worshipers. Below the floor resided the mummified remains of members of the confraternity of death.

Our guide showed us a glass case where slivers of the relics resided. Laurie and I, to the bewilderment of the faithful around us, crouched down on hands and knees to get a closer look, but could see nothing.

Suddenly our guide appeared beside me.

"I have a surprise for you" he whispered, and handed me a card with the icon of Chrysanthus and Daria on it. I thanked him and continued to weep.

"Well, come on, I said I have a surprise."

Laurie and I looked at each other and followed him to the other side of the altar. Laurie grasped my hand tightly, and led me to a table where two men were seated, talking to our escort. He procured another key and beckoned us to follow.

Consumed by tears, I stumbled through the door and down a red-carpeted stairway decorated with a photo of the Pope and cloth banners. At the end of a white marble staircase, in a room behind a black gate, lay the object of my search. Among the prized holy chalices and plates, the sculptures of angels, Jesus and Mary used during the Easter procession, lay the relics of Saints Chrysanthus and Daria.

Overcome by emotion, I again fell to my knees in admiration and respect for what lay before me. The spirit of Saint Chrysanthus enveloped me. I experienced a profound peace.

"I don't have any more surprises" our guide murmured. Speechless, I continued to gaze at the bust of Chrysanthus, his eyes looking to heaven.

"I think your saint wanted you to come," he continued, seemingly pleased now that I had stopped dampening the floor with my tears. "You are very lucky."

"I know," I replied, "Very lucky."

After fifteen minutes of personal communion, our guide escorted us out. As we slowly walked outside of the Basilica, the soft sounds of church bells floated through the evening breeze.

RETURN OF LA BRAVA

ETHEL F. MUSSEN

"*D*o you believe in reincarnation?" Roger asked me, as we walked along the ancient stones of this spur of the Via Appia near Monopoli. In Puglia, the jumble of cultures and history readily evokes feelings of déjà vu. Although reincarnation was a concept better suited to mystical Roger than to pragmatic me, my thirty-five-year-old search for the medieval warrior woman lent itself to such a possibility.

The tantalizing leads I'd gotten from newspaper archives only hinted at the story I'd once cut out of the paper. Datelined L'Aquila, February 1972, it read: "Archaeologists here are puzzled at finding a seven-foot skeleton of a woman on Monte Della Laga in the Appenines. The grave is about 750 years old. The woman is holding a mace and her head has been severed." My original clipping had included something about armor and Frederick, the

Holy Roman Emperor. I had kept the little story and was intrigued enough to seek her remains at the museum in L'Aquila in 1983, but nobody seemed to know of the findings or such an exhibit. I lost my crumbling copy of the article, but never forgot its "Tall Old Woman."

Now I was en route to join a group of travel writers to explore Puglia, but I opted for a few additional days in Rome to search again for my beheaded lady. If I were lucky, she had been moved to a museum or study center in Rome.

My quest for information led me through the tumultuous events of the Middle Ages. The gradual decay of the Roman and Byzantine Empires into communities overrun by Normans and Lombards from the North and Arabs from the East resulted in the chaos of wars, conquests and resettlement. Meanwhile, powerful Popes promoted the spread of Christianity and overrode many factional struggles.

In the mid-twelfth century, Frederick Hohenstauffern, called Barbarossa or Red Beard, became the new Holy Roman Emperor. He was ambitious and swept into Italy with his supporters to unify pieces of the old Empire as they pushed to conquer the Middle East and Jerusalem. He confronted the Papal power of Alexander III, however, who ruled his own states throughout Italy and exerted vast religious authority all over Europe. When Frederick installed German governors in the autonomous cities of Northern Italy, the resistant Lombard League, or Guelphs, arose, loyal to the Pope in Rome and ready to defy the Germans.

Their resistance was aided by widespread malaria at the Battle of Legnano in 1176, and Frederick eventually signed pacts of non-interference with the Pope and the Lombard League.

Based on the approximate dates of the grave belonging to the "Tall Old Woman," I decided it was not Barbarossa who defeated my lady warrior but more likely his successor, Frederick II. Born in 1197, he had already achieved fame by 1220 as *Stupor Mundi* (Wonder of the World), the brilliant young King of Sicily and heir to the Emperor's crown. Educated, multi-lingual, and as ambitious as his model, he strode across Italy, establishing schools and universities throughout his domains, marrying and bedding beautiful and endowed women, and building fortresses with stout walls and broad lookouts through the land to defend against the dreaded Saracens. Yet, contrary to the Pope's desire to ruthlessly eradicate every trace of the "infidel," Frederick II preferred diplomacy, conferred with the Sultan and acquired the Kingdom of Jerusalem by marriage.

The more I learned, the more I guessed that my warrior woman had lost her head to Frederick II when the hero of the south became the scourge of the north. I began to fantasize again about the living woman, trying to picture her life and death. And since Frederick II was so revered in Puglia, I hoped my journey there would hold some answers.

Suddenly, on a warm sunny day, a vision arose before me as I listened to the strains of Khatchaturian's mournful music. Pale, lashless eyes gazed at me, her long hair streamed about her broad shoulders, and in that moment of epiphany I dubbed her *La Brava*, "The Brave One." I had my vision and needed no other name.

Surely she must have joined the men about her when they gathered with the rest of the Lombard League to protest Frederick II's domination. Like other fighting women of the period, she donned chain mail and fought to defend rights, virtue and property.

Other women were celebrated and recorded, but of my nameless heroine, there was no trace. In the eleventh century, Matilda of Tuscany conducted wars to defend the papacy's holdings in Italy. At the same time, Sikelgaita fought beside her husband, Robert Guiscard, in Puglia. She rode at the head of the troops urging them to "Be Men!" as he conquered southern Italy including Naples from the Adriatic to the Mediterranean.

The fifteenth century nuns of the convent of Santa Apollonia in Florence commissioned Castagno to paint frescoes depicting the earlier Battle of Legnaia with those sisters who had donned armor to resist rape by invading troops and fought "virily" to defend their virginity and faith. Danish, Saxon and Viking women joined their men, both as invaders and defenders, and oddly fought bare-breasted "to frighten their opponents," while the Norman Isabel of Conches rode armed as a knight in 1090.

Spanish, Portuguese, French, English, Chinese and Mohammedan queens and noblewomen, alone or with their husbands, defended their cities and castles. Although history describes them as armored, they are often portrayed in statuaries and paintings in fine dress. Queens Eleanor of Castile and Eleanor of Aquitaine rode like men when they accompanied their husbands on Crusades to the Holy Land. In the fifteenth century, Jeanne d'Arc commanded troops and fought wearing the solid metal armor of the time.

But of my lady, her grave opened 750 years after her burial, chain mail covering her bones, mace and severed head at her side—*no name*, no battle record.

In Rome, she abruptly appeared, not as a specter, but tall and animated, squeezing her way past diners at a sidewalk café, rapt in conversation with a diminutive companion. Vigorous, golden-haired, trailing a scarf over her thin summer tunic, she strode purposefully toward the *ristorante* we'd discovered just the night before. Owned by a small, brunette couple from L'Aquila, they proudly mounted a poster of the Fountain Wall with its ninety-nine spouting heads to remind them of home. Could this tall golden-haired girl be related to them?

Even as she disappeared into the kitchen, I knew that our journey to Puglia must fill in more details. Answers did indeed lie in the castles of Frederick II. First at Castel del Monte, that brooding hilltop octagon of stone meant to invoke the mystical oneness of God. Beneath his portrait, a time-line detailed the rise of Frederick II from birth in 1197, through boyhood to maturity, with an account of his assumptions to power, his marriages and acquisitions.

There, one brief entry was dedicated to 1237, when he was welcomed back in Sicily just before going to marry Yolanda de Brienne, the heiress of Jerusalem. He was unfortunately diverted north to put down a new rebellion of the Lombard League. This he accomplished radically and severely, leaving plans for a new fortress to replace the destroyed community. He named the fortress L'Aquila—the Eagle—in honor of the black double eagle of the Hohenstauffern arms. He installed the gold and black banner to remind the Italians of their German Emperor. Thus I found the sad date of La Brava's battle and death listed as a minor aberration in the litany of Frederick II's majestic good deeds.

Final closure came at Castel Svevo outside Oria—a recycled Norman keep, beloved by Frederick II and constantly in use since his rebuilding, sometimes happily, sometimes brutally. A larger-than-life bronze Frederick II stands guard outside the building, his robes falling to his ankles, overlooking the valley and the hills. Inside, the latest owners have left a legacy for the public to view: sparsely furnished rooms from different periods, portraits on the walls of medieval and Renaissance nobles, and standing armor displayed against the walls of the Great Hall.

Then one enters the Arms Hall—two stories high—with clusters of lances in the supporting columns, leading to a single faceless stand bearing the tunic and chain mail of the thirteenth century. On one wall, two red and white Crusader shields gleamed, faced on the opposite wall by three Hohenstauffern shields of black eagles on ochre ground. Two trompe l'oeil scrolls recount the history of Castel Svevo. Another display in the next hallway lays out the family tree from Barbarossa through Frederick II's marriages and liaisons and resulting offspring.

As I stood alone, the hall around me became animated with imagined action. I examined again the two red shields and the maces on either side—one, a straight pointed club with black spikes at the tip, and the other the shorter club with iron chain attached and a black spiked round ball at the end. A long sword divides them. Then, magically, the battle erupted:

La Brava in chain mail, her left hand holding a round shield before her breast, standing her position in the rocky crags among her companions, her hair streaming as her helmet falls to the ground while she flails and twirls the mace against warriors holding the detested ochre shields. And suddenly an unseen assailant strikes her unprotected head from her shoulders with a long sword. When the battle ends, loving arms bury my lady and her weapons on the mountain where she fell.

Did the bones crumble when they finally met air and sun in 1972? Did they reassemble into a new being, leaving the blackened chain mail to hang on a museum wall? Did the dark-haired couple from L'Aquila welcome a strange golden-haired child into their life thirty-five years ago? Was it her spirit I saw in my vision, her body I saw in Rome? Do I believe in reincarnation, Roger? Oh yes, I believe the spirit of *La Brava* lives and breathes in the world today.

LINKS TO PUGLIA'S PAST

CONNIE BURKE

"Quindi il golf e anche l'immaginazione del ritorno alle origin."
"Golf helps the imagination go back to its origins."
—Lino Patruno, editor of *La Gazzeta del Mezzogiorno*.

*S*tanding over my ball on the first tee of a Puglian golf course, I was distracted by a delicate tiny white *pet-thalia* (butterfly in ancient Greek) landing gently on the soft grass to the left of my tee. I turned to look and for the barest instant, I felt a connection between myself and the ancient Greeks.

You don't have to be a mythographer to sense what always was. In the realm of sport, Puglia offers the same excitement today as it did in the past. On the plains of Tessaglia, from the seventh century to the third century BCE, Greek javelin and discus throwers came to challenge their opponents in open fields curtained by the leafy boughs of pine, oak and olive. Their victories depended on their ability to visualize the shape and height of their throw, distance to target and wind direction—not unlike golf today.

Riva dei Tessali (The Shore of Thessaly) Golf Course takes its name from its historic past. The golf course is in the heart of what was once called Magna Graecia (Great Greece), for Puglia was colonized by Greeks before it was conquered by Rome.

In the seventh century BCE, led by Phalanthos, Spartan women sent their illegitimate children across the Ionian Sea to live as free citizens in what legend called *paradeisos*. Other Greek colonists established settlements throughout the southern region of Italy and Sicily. Greek heroes Theseus, Odysseus and Aeneus proudly entered her ports; Plato and Pythagorus reasoned under the shade of her ancient trees.

It is still a *paradeisos*. Created in 1968, Riva dei Tessali Golf Course is a 5,960 meter, 18-hole par 71 championship course and the traditional venue for the Puglia and Basilicata Open (now in its twenty-second year). Situated in a dense stand of Aleppo pines, the golf course borders the Ionian coastline and groves upon groves of orange and olive trees.

The Aleppo pines predate the earliest Greek settlements in the region. Though the ancient Greeks planted the olive trees, the pines are thought to come from Syria, their seeds carried unwittingly by migratory birds that still come to winter here. Even today, it takes little time for planted seeds to sprout, as the soil is still very fertile and the climate mild all year round.

The strong scent of pine permeates the air on this first *buca* (hole). Holding my driver upright with the club-head on the ground, I envisioned a javelin thrower holding a ten-foot thrusting spear with an iron tip and butt, his naked body covered in olive oil. He stares into the distance, into an open field of dry wavering grass. He knows that a good throw is determined by the trajectory he imparts, as well as the aerodynamic behavior of the spear. Like the golfer, he craves transcendence as he watches his spear soar to greater and further heights.

I, too, craved transcendence. I wanted to see the titanium-compound core of that little white dimpled ball shoot down the fairway of the first *buca*, a par 4 dog-leg to the right. But I realized I had the wrong club. A good drive would probably land my ball in a bed of dried pine needles. Like many of the holes at Riva dei Tessali, this hole required precision and a shorter drive. Although it was hot, I wasn't excited about spending most of the eighteen-hole journey off the fairways in the deep shade.

Play safe, I reminded myself. I pulled out a five wood, swung at the ball and watched it land short of the turn. Satisfied, I started walking down the fairway to my ball.

You don't have to dig deep into the soft green fairways of Riva dei Tessali to discover her past. You might not hear the rumble of war elephants trampling through battle-stained fields. But looking down the narrow fairway, you can certainly sense the puissance of a thousand legions marching over the dried grasses of a

Puglia well-before-Christ.

In the early third century BCE, with the threat of the mighty legions of Rome at their borders, the Greeks of Taras asked Pyrrhus, King of Epirus, for help. They weren't disappointed.

Disembarking from ships onto the Ionian shores of Tessaglia, the King's troops advanced with 20,000 phalanxes, 500 shield-bearing peltasts, 2,000 archers, 3,000 elite cavalry from Thessaly and twenty war elephants. The Romans mobilized eight legions totaling about 80,000 soldiers, divided into four armies. The Greek army prevailed and the Battle of Heraclea was won by Pyrrhus. But the casualties were high. The brave men of Thessaly fell like tree leaves in autumn.

Subsequently, after the Battle of Beneventum, Pyrrhus, tall and proud, with sunbeams crossed along his mighty breastplate and plumes of golden horse-hair flowing from the peak of his helmet, left Italy. His departure led to the fall of Magna Graecia and the dominance of Rome in the Italian peninsula.

The Greeks, like the Roman legions, are gone now; their echoed cries of battle replaced by a gentle wind whispering through the tall, dry, July grasses of a Puglian fairway. The pines recall the tall spears lifted high above the warriors' heads before charging into battle. Sand traps neatly sculpted around each hole cover the holes where sheep once dug to seek shelter from prevailing winds. The landscape is quiet now; the plains of Tessaglia blanketed in rich green bermuda grass.

On the Ionian coast north of Taranto, the narrow fairways of the first eight holes of Riva dei Tessali meander through the tall pines whose crowns, while offering cool shade in the hottest days of a waning June, often interfere with the trajectory of the ball. But the back nine opens up and the golfer is welcomed by wider fairways, a cool breeze coming off the Ionian Sea and a legion of orange trees.

According to Angelo Zella, President of Riva Dei Tessali-Metaponto Golf Club, "Puglia has the advantage of having beautiful landscapes as well as cultural and artistic fortunes . . . *che in piu ha il supporto di bellezze pasesaggistiche e del partimonio cuturale ed artistico che privilegiano la nostra regione.*"

Cultural fortunes abound under all Puglian fairways. Acaya Golf Club near Lecce is spread out between Castle Acaya, the Adriatic Sea and the nature reserve of Cesine. From the club house golfers look onto two Basilian crypts built by Basilian monks who migrated from Constantinople in the tenth century CE in a second wave of Greek colonization.

The San Domenico Golf Club and the nine-hole Coccaro Golf Club lie near the archeological site of Egnazia, once a significant port for trade between the settlements of Magna Graecia and other Mediterranean lands. Though the nine-hole Coccaro Golf Club sits on a hilly terrain, San Domenico hugs the Adriatic Sea. No trees delimit San Domenico's fairways, but the familiar twisted bark of a few age-old olive trees meld with myrtle, sage and thyme.

Founded in 1996, the Barialto Golf Club is carved out of

olive groves. Palm trees and five lakes add to the landscape of this green oasis outside of Puglia's industrial capital, Bari.

The newest course, Metaponto Golf Club, lies near some of the most ancient ruins of Magna Graecia. The town of Metaponto in the province of Basilicata is only a ten-minute drive from Riva dei Tessali. Its name, of Greek origin, means "between two bridges." Wide fairways lined by cactuses, undulating greens, lakes and channels amplify the picturesque landscape of the Lucania region. Three ancient temples dedicated to Apollo Lycio, Hera and Athena dramatize the agricultural terrain.

Playing a round of golf on any of Puglia's courses, one senses the ancient history and culture buried beneath the fairways. And at Riva dei Tessali, whose name derives from "butterfly," *petthalii* grace the greens.

PUGLIA AND MIDDLE-EARTH

THOMAS R. HARRELL

f the hobbits of J.R.R. Tolkein's imagination could be persuaded to leave their beloved Shire and travel south (admittedly a difficult proposition, for hobbits greatly dislike travel), I believe they might find a second home in Puglia. I even hazard to guess that a few intrepid hobbits, seduced by the bounty of Puglia's farms, its unique architecture and warm welcome, might just stay in Puglia and embrace *la dolce vita* (the sweet life).

For those unfamiliar with hobbits, the diminutive heroes of the eponymous novel and *Lord of the Rings* trilogy (*Il Signore degli Anelli* in Italian), they are about half our size, wear no shoes because their feet grow naturally leathery soles and thick warm hair, and love to laugh, especially after meals (they love to eat). This is a short version, if you will pardon the pun.

My first thought on seeing the famous *trulli* houses of Puglia was of hobbits. No hobbit could resist these charming homes, which so wonderfully evoke their own comfortable style of hobbit architecture, whose "chief remaining peculiarity" is a fondness for round windows and doors. The whimsical *trulli* houses, so similarly designed, must seem a perfect spot for a rest and bite (or two) to eat.

Trulli are built of stone with conical roofs of narrowing concentric rings, and look like an upside-down ice cream cone on a square base. They often have small round windows burrowing through the thick stone walls, and arched doorways; they are whitewashed inside and out. In the *trulli* capital of Puglia, Alberobello, the *trulli* seem to grow like mushrooms after a rainstorm on the town's twin hillsides.

I was fascinated by the tale of *trulli* history, and I believe the pastoral hobbits would also appreciate the genius of Puglia's farmers in the Middle Ages. It is believed the *trulli* were first built around 1500 CE by peasants migrating from Puglia's shrinking forests to new farms, often not completely of their own accord. The new farmers had to clear the fields of the abundant local limestone rocks and build homes where little wood was available. *Trulli* were the clever solution to both problems. Originally constructed of irregular stones piled *a seco* (dry, or without mortar), history has it that once the local landlords realized how easily the *trulli* could be demolished prior to the arrival of the royal tax man (who counted the number of houses), and then rebuilt, they forbade the use of mortar. Only after royal intervention in 1797 was the use of mortar allowed.

My own *trullo*, which I shared with Roger, another full-size human, was located midway up the west slope of Alberobello's *trulli* district. It was a modest but tidy one-cone corner house with a dutch door—several inches too short for a pair of six-footers—and a trio of small round windows tunneling through the walls of the tiny bathroom, alcove kitchen and bedroom. Although no larger than many American living rooms, the *trullo* felt remarkably spacious and light inside with the high conical ceiling, whitewashed walls and rustic furniture. Nonetheless, Roger and I soon learned to walk with a slight stoop through the doorways and to be especially vigilant in the bathroom, where a heavy beam separated the toilet from the unwary. Although I could not in good conscience recommend a *trullo* vacation to a basketball team, it suits the average human well and would be perfect for a visiting hobbit.

No matter how charming the accommodations, neither man nor hobbit can live without food; indeed, hobbits are especially fond of eating (they prefer at least six meals a day) and would relish Puglia's bounteous meals.

Puglia has cultivated olives and grapes for thousands of years, and its farms also grow cherries, walnuts, pomegranates, eggplant and a laundry list of other delectables. Fresh seafood is common, though hobbits never touch the stuff. I remember with particular nostalgia one meal we enjoyed at the *masseria* Tenute Pedale, an organic farm with tourist accommodations in the plain below the Castel del Monte. Lunch began with *bruschetta* covered in fresh-picked tomatoes and local olive oil, followed by eggplant parmigiana and zucchini, carrots with olive oil and capers, *focaccia* with roasted tomatoes, homemade lamb and pork sausages, mozzarella made that very morning, as well as a fresh ricotta that literally melted in the mouth. Local wines were liberally served. And, just when I swore I couldn't devour another morsel, we were served sweet cherries from the garden for dessert. It would have been rude not to partake! Even hobbit hero Bilbo Baggins, a great lover of food, would have enthusiastically approved.

Hobbits are hospitable, willing to share a last seed-cake with an unexpected guest, even though their own stomachs are rumbling, and would certainly appreciate this aspect of Puglia. Throughout the trip I was struck by the generosity and warmth of Puglia's people, from an afternoon spent with singer Al Bano Carrisi (hobbits would love his miniature horses) to a train car I shared with three Puglians on my way to Rome. The three, a newlywed couple and proud mother-in-law, spoke little English, which is to say more than my Italian. Still, they insisted on sharing their chocolate cookies and Italian gossip magazine, which was most welcome on the seven-hour trip. By Campania we had bonded over food and fashion, and by Rome we parted companions, language differences forgotten.

J.R.R. Tolkein wrote to W.H. Auden that "Middle-earth is not an imaginary world . . . . The theatre of my tale is this earth, the one in which we now live, but the historical period is imaginary." From "this earth," Tolkein was able to spin fantastic stories of courage and adventure, mixed with humor. Puglia has experienced nearly as many invasions, conquests and historic battles as Middle-earth, unfortunately all too real, and has its own rich legacy of tales and legends.

Although it is doubtful Tolkein ever visited Puglia, he could have had Puglians in mind when he said "I am a Hobbit (in all but size). I like gardens, trees and unmechanized farmlands; I smoke a pipe and like good plain food (unrefrigerated), but detest French cooking . . . ." He pictured the rural England of his childhood, but a wandering hobbit might just prefer a cozy *trullo* with olive trees and a tidy vineyard in front and a garden behind, far removed from fog and rain (and the threat of unwelcome adventure). You will find me next door.

Vini Pugliesi

Eleanor Shannon

"Unfortunately, Signora, the Count is not at home," announced a man from the open window of his car. In front of me was a sign that said: *Conte Spagnoletti Zeuli* (Count Spagnoletti Zeuli). I was confused. *Is there really a Count? I thought to myself, Is this the winery I have been looking for? Where is my writers' group? Has the tour already begun?*

I leaned out of my car window and explained that I was looking for the winery and my group. With a broad smile, the man answered, "*Fantastico!* I am Antonio. I have been here waiting for your group myself. They were supposed to arrive half an hour ago. Do you know where they are?"

"No! I wish I did!" I exclaimed, laughing out loud and thinking how funny it was that Antonio was looking for the group, too. Nothing is ever linear in Italy. Things tend to move sideways, backwards and even upside down. I gave him our guide Marilù's phone number. He called and found that the bus had actually gotten lost and, by mistake, had ended up at the other end of the estate, a few kilometers away. Ironically, that was actually where the wine cellar was and where the tour would begin. Antonio offered to lead me there. In a lovely, sideways manner, things were falling into place.

As I followed Antonio on a dusty road through rows of grapevines, I was curious about what kinds of wine the Count made. The name Puglia or Apulia derives from a Latin word used by the Romans, A-*pluvia*, meaning lack of rain or aridness. This area is known for its torrid heat and lack of rain. As a result, the vineyards have very high yields (four to five times the grapes per acre typical of other regions) and the grapes generally have a strong flavor and high alcohol content.

In fact, this region, like Sicily, has long been known for producing vast quantities of relatively low-quality wine. There are about 100,000 hectares (250,000 acres) under cultivation yielding 185 million gallons of wine annually, three-quarters of which is sold in bulk to "spice up" Tuscan or other northern Italian wines, or as a basis for vermouth.

There are no DOCG wines produced in Puglia. (Top Italian wines are labeled DOCG: Original Location Certified and Guaranteed, meaning that the wine meets certain stringent qualifications and that the grapes and the wine are produced in a designated area.) By comparison, the entire Chianti region, half of

Tuscany, is DOCG.

Although Puglia has twenty-five DOC (Certified Original Location) areas, a less stringent geographical designation, only 2-3% of the region's wine is DOC. The vast majority is considered table wine. Some twenty-five to thirty percent of the table wine consumed in Italy comes from Puglia.

I knew that Castel Del Monte is one of the best known DOC areas in Puglia, second only to Salice Salentino in terms of reputation. The area is hilly and elevated above sea level, meaning that it is not as hot as the nearly three-quarters of Puglian vineyards that lie in the plains along the sea.

The tour was underway when I arrived. Michele (pronounced Mi-KAY-lay), our guide, explained some of the technical aspects of the wine making process.

"The red wine ferments in this large steel vat in about a week at 30° C, but the white has to ferment more slowly at 17-20° to protect its delicate bouquet." The technical description seemed appropriate to the room we were standing in; it was filled with modern steel equipment, hoses, bright lights, precision measurement devices and had a cold concrete floor.

The next room had a different feel, darker, older and more traditional. Michele went on, "These are the vats where we put the wine for aging once the fermentation process is complete. As you can see, these are old vats made of iron. Inside, there are so many layers of varnish that the surface feels like glass."

Then, Michele led us outside into the bright light and heat of the day. We crossed a courtyard and began descending a stone ramp, about ten feet wide, made of huge blocks of tufa, a soft yellowish volcanic rock typical of Puglia. At the bottom of the ramp, forty feet below ground, we found ourselves in an enormous *cantina* (wine cellar). The walls and ceiling of the cellar were perfectly squared off and filled with hundreds of bottles neatly stacked on their sides so that only their round bottoms were visible.

It seemed we had arrived in the sanctum sanctorum. Michele beamed, "This is the Count's *cantina*. It was originally the quarry for all of the tufa stone used to build the estate's *masseria* (fortified farmhouse). The stone was cut and transported up the ramp, leaving a vast empty underground space behind: a perfect *cantina*. The cellar maintains a constant year round temperature of 17° C with 95% humidity, ideal for aging and storing wine."

Michele continued, "The Count, himself, is very involved in all parts of the wine making process. He decides which wines to make and which grapes to grow. In June and July every year, we actually go out into the fields with him, inspect the vines, and decide which grapes we are going to pick and use for making each kind of wine."

"What kind of grapes does the Count grow?" I asked.

"For red and rosé wines, he grows *Troia* (also called *Nero di Troia*) grapes, said to have been brought to Puglia from Troy by the Greeks. He also grows *Montepulciano* and *Cabernet* grapes. For white wines, he grows *Fiano di Puglia* along with two other varieties: *Pampanuto* and *Bombino*."

The cool shadows of the cellar fell around me as Michele spoke. The place had an inherent element of pure Puglian practicality: nothing was wasted and no extra effort expended. The stones had been cut and carried out, creating space for a cellar.

At the same time, there was a feeling of mystery and of spiritual connection to the earth: grapes brought from ancient Troy, vines rooted deeply in the soil, a cellar born of eons-old volcanic rock, wine making methods of ancestors long dead, a *cantina* with precisely the right temperature for aging the wine, and managing all of it, the Count himself.

Michele led us over to an old oaken barrel-shaped vat. "This is very special." He explained, "We choose *Troia* grapes to be fermented and aged in this vat. They never touch steel." He continued proudly, "We produce a very small amount of specialty wine this way, according to completely traditional methods. The Count has named this wine *Rinzacco.*"

The name sounded exotic. I was wishing the Count, tall, with dark hair and chiseled aristocratic features, would appear from the shadows, uncork a bottle there in the cellar and pour me a glass. *"Signora," he would whisper softly, "Come here for a moment. I would like to offer you a glass of my Rinzacco. Will you do me the honor of tasting it?"*

Instead, it was Michele who began uncorking bottles in the tasting room. He first offered us a red, *Pezzalruca* (50% *Montepulciano* and 50% *Troia*). Next we tasted the Count's rosé *Mezzana* (20% *Troia* and 80% *Montepulciano*) and, a white, *Jody*

(100% *Fiano*). Finally, he poured glasses of the precious *Rinzacco*. The taste was full and smooth, as delicious as I had expected. I drank in not only the flavor, but the experiences of the day: the frenzy of my arrival, the tour with Michele, the *cantina*, and now the wines.

As he poured, Michele explained that the Count's family has been making Castel del Monte wines since the sixteen hundreds, but all the current wines have been developed within the last thirty years. The Count only has about a hundred hectares (250 acres) in cultivation. He is part of an entrepreneurial trend in the region toward the production of low quantities of high-quality, boutique wines. The efforts of vintners have begun paying off as a small number of Puglian wines have been recognized for excellence and value.

In 2007, the prestigious Gambero Rosso guide awarded Puglia five of its top "three glass" awards, all for red wines. In 2008, the region won seven of these. Conte Spagnoletti Zeuli was not a winner but another Castel Del Monte wine maker, Torrevento, was. Progress is slow but steady for growers/producers even though in comparison to other regions like Tuscany, Puglia lags far behind. For example, Tuscany won sixty-five of the Italian total of three hundred and five "three glass" awards.

Three of the winning Puglian wines in 2008 were made from *Primitivo* grapes (from vineyards toward the south of Puglia near Taranto and Salice Salentino), two from *Negro Amaro* (Bari and Lecce) and two from *Nero di Troia* (Castel Del Monte, north of

Bari, and Alberobello, south of Bari). All of these grapes are considered native to southern Italy since they were brought or developed by the very first inhabitants of the region: Messapians and Greeks. In some cases, the wine is made from one kind of grape, but in other cases grapes like *Malvasia Nera* (also considered native to Puglia) or *Montepulciano* or *Sangiovese* are mixed in.

Even though the reds rank as the best of Puglian wines, there are a number of up-and-coming rosés and whites. The Leone Di Castris vineyard from Salice Salentino, for example, produces award-winning whites as well as reds.

The town of Locorotondo in the Itria Valley is also considered an important producer of top quality whites, one of which I sampled when I first arrived in Puglia. It was a *Bombino*, light with an almost greenish or straw color. The most planted native Puglian varietals are *Bombino*, *Bianco d'Alessano*, *Fiano* and *Verdeca*, but they are often grown alongside *Chardonnay* and *Sauvignon* grapes.

The Count, like many vintners in Puglia, is building on centuries-old wine traditions to develop new wines and to change the region's reputation for selling everyday table wine in bulk. Puglia has already been called the "new Tuscany" and maybe one day it will be. After all, it was not long ago that olive oil became a chic alternative to butter, and Chianti moved from being a "poor cousin" sold in baskets to a top international competitor in the world of wine.

As I was driving back to Milano a few days later, I saw signs on the highway for Andria. *Is the Count at home today?* I wondered. *Should I call Antonio to try to arrange a last minute visit?*

No, I decided. *Not on this trip.* I preferred for the Count to remain as he was: mythical and mysterious. I had packed a treasured bottle of *Rinzacco* in my bag. On some cold, winter night, I would open it and allow a sensuous flood of memories to return: the intense heat of a late June morning, winding roads through ancient olive groves, a cool, dark *cantina*, a first taste of the wines of Puglia, and a quest for an illusive Italian Count.

SPEAKING IN HANDS

JOANNA BIGGAR

*T*t all began with Sophia Loren. Growing up on the beaches of Southern California neither slim nor blond, I decided I could become like her—dark, sultry, busty and able to use both mouth and hips to considerable advantage. Naturally, dark, handsome men would fall at my feet, but I would brush past them leaving a trail of pithy remarks in my rapier-like Italian.

I revisited that fantasy a few months ago while preparing to go to southern Italy and again watching her starring role in the 1961 classic, *Two Women*. Somehow I had not turned into Sophia Loren and my rapid-fire Italian was still sputtering. But I had become a writer, and seeing the film again I found there was a new lesson there, the equivalent of an advanced degree in communication: Loren's smoldering eyes, quivering mouth, defiant hips, rebellious hair and the graphic hands that covered her own despair, tenderly soothed her wounded daughter, or angrily sliced the air in front of a startled Nazi officer's face.

The full import of that lesson hit me on a graffiti-covered tram south of Naples—Loren's hometown. From the opposite end of the rollicking car I had an unimpeded view of a man talking to his seatmate. His physical characteristics, even the ceaseless movement of his lips and facial expressions dim in my memory as I reconstruct the ballet of his hands: drawing pictures, conducting a symphony, slicing bread, making tiny circles of his fingers, as if sipping tea with royalty. It was an astonishing performance, and it struck me then that maybe I could speak Italian after all. Despite my third faltering attempt to teach myself the language, I was still making fatal verbal mistakes, mixing up pasta (*calzone*), for example, with socks (*calzini*). And decades older than Loren in *Two Women*, it seemed prudent not to call on certain body parts to express myself. But hands? Certainly I, too, could speak in hands.

Language coaches, I figured, should be everywhere, and began my personal, if unscientific, search. It took a while for it to dawn on me that speaking in hands, like much else in this part of Italy, was a gender thing.

As I settled into Alberobello, in Puglia, with my writers' group, I started looking for role models of expression. Early every morning, I went to "my" cafe where I greeted the jovial proprietor Giovanni with my hearty "*buongiorno*" and "*un cappuccino per favore,"* one finger waving tepidly in the air, then having exhausted my ready Italian, sat in a quiet corner with my note-book to observe. I was never disappointed.

One morning two men came in and continued their animat-ed conversation just above my head; words, yes, but more it was a wild dance of hands, sweeping lightly, making tiny, circular pas de deux, leaping to heaven before becoming a twirling *tarantella* that ended with each one jabbing a finger into the other's chest. Mesmerized, and assuming I was completely invisible, I was startled when one of them glanced down at me and said some-thing . . . in Italian. Stunned, I looked behind the counter to Giovanni's wife for a sign. *Show me the moves,* I silently begged her. But she smiled beatifically, and wordless as usual, slightly raised only one eyebrow.

"Non parlo Italiano," I replied, adding only the half-formed shrug of a linguistic nincompoop.

As I became aware of it, I saw the pattern repeat. Seeking respite from the mid-day sun I slipped into a pizza restaurant in a *trullo* a few doors from mine. Seated next to an Italian family with mother, father, two young boys and an older girl, I was entranced by their animated conversation. Not that I could understand it. Until, that is, the boy Francesco, about eight, began to tell a story. His hands moved in parallel tracks, dividing and conquering the air, then weaving through currents of narra-tive until they smashed together triumphantly. He laughed. His father gestured. His mother and sister laughed too, hands still by their plates.

You're not helping my communication skills. I felt like lecturing them in scolding school-marmish tones, my imaginary conversation wild with gesticulation. Instead I smiled knowingly, as if I got it, words and all, as if I weren't a floundering foreign writer, as if I could speak Italian.

The notion of a gender/gesture divide continued to haunt me. A couple of nights later, I repaired to a favorite wine bar with outdoor tables where one could enjoy the shade and the passing parade as day melted into warm, pleasant evening. Wine in hand, I peered through the leaves of large flowering potted plants to observe the legs of two park benches. Beneath them were several pairs of shoes—men's shoes as it turned out—but I didn't need to see them to know who they were. Everywhere in my vision I saw hands, only hands, pointing, rolling, ruffling the air, punctuating the rising night. I stood briefly to verify what I already knew: this was another of the retired men's "clubs" that gathered in cafes, on benches and sidewalks everywhere to joke, laugh, reminisce, share stories.

But where were the ladies? As if in reply, at that very moment a group of three older women came from the street and sat at a table not too far from me. Church bells began to ring as I watched them unfold into the evening. They relaxed, setting their shopping bags on the ground and ordering wine, drawing cigarettes from their purses and leaning into each other to talk. *At last I'll see how to speak like a woman*, I thought, and discreetly pulled out my notebook. I watched for forty minutes as they jabbered and laughed; their words, if I could have heard them, as foreign to me as if they had been speaking in tongues, their hands, save to summon the waiter or straighten their hair, mute on the table.

Why was this? In response to my own question, I began to observe closely the women around me. Young girls, in the ubiquitous uniform of jeans and tank tops, swayed down the street holding a cell phone in one hand, a purse in the other. Young mothers held the hands of children, pushed prams and lugged the paraphernalia of motherhood. Women of all ages carried shopping bags, often many at a time, and sometimes hauled carts. I thought back to other women I'd met here, to Giovanni's wife whose hands were either making coffee or drying glasses, to our tour guide Marilù, whose hands were wrapped around a microphone as her tongue wrapped around the stories of Puglia she was telling. That was it then: these women's hands were either too full, or too busy, to "talk."

This insight, however, was no help at all to my dilemma. With Sophia Loren-style body language and hand signals definitely out of reach, and the local women offering no alternatives, it meant I'd have to do some cross-over male-type gesturing or hit the phrase book harder.

I decided on a combination approach, which got tested very soon. In the medieval town of Oria I encountered Pino Malva, guide, historian and local history writer. At about five feet four, he wore a wide panama hat, large-frame glasses, a pin-striped shirt unbuttoned half-way down his chest, yellowish pants, and chain-smoked, talked and joked non-stop while he led us through the narrow streets. Of course, his hands were a study in perpetual motion. Soon we found ourselves inside a stone-vaulted restaurant where the food, ambiance and dress of the servers were straight from the fourteenth century. Under its gothic roof, Malva addressed us, his palms turning in and out in swooping movements that ended like a flock of birds coming in for a landing. Finished, he sat down at the wooden plank table right next to me and the conversation in both modes continued unabated.

At one point I asked, "Are you also a poet?" and expected a reply worthy of his flamboyance. Instead he asked in return, "Why, are you?" I meant to match eloquence with eloquence, but his act was too much to follow, let alone emulate. Instead, I sat dumb, tongue and hand-tied.

That condition followed me throughout Puglia. Oh, I could still order my morning *cappuccino* or ask my way to the train station, but I felt stuck somewhere in Lesson 7 of *Beginning Italian*. I felt immobile.

Then, a strangely liberating thing happened: I got sick.

As my husband and I drove into northern Puglia after the workshop, I began to feel hot. This was not surprising as the temperature hovered around 40° C and went up from there. By the time we pulled into the ancient port city of Manfredonia, I knew I was making my own small contribution to global warming.

Under the shady roof of a restaurant terrace full of sea breezes, I watched a foursome near us—a man and three women—through a wash of feverish haze. That night I revisited the lunch, dreaming myself into a starring role.

The man, with grizzled gray hair pulled back into a ponytail, flexed his biceps often, his naked arms easily visible beneath his bright blue muscle shirt. Across from him sat his wife, a small, quiet woman in a black dress. Next to them were two other women, middle-aged travelers I guessed who became a captive audience. The man spoke in a loud, sing-song voice, accompanied by his arms and hands, which whirled relentlessly, as if propellers to launch his endless story. Occasionally one of the women's voices could be heard in timid soprano counterpoint, but would quickly give way. Once the younger of the two women let her hand rise and fall a few times, like a fish trying to break surface, only to retreat below. I could stand it no more. I rose, majestically to be sure, and confronted them. "Don't let him get away with this, signore," I said. "Speak up! Speak back! Use your hands!" My Italian was flawless of course and my arms whipped around in windmill-fashion while I twirled like a dervish.

Soon, intimidated by me I was sure, they all rose and disappeared. Then I saw my reflection. I had become an octopus flailing about in an aquarium, silent bubbles slipping from my beak. Humans, including my four lunch-mates, stood outside the glass, gawking.

It's probably fair to say my transformation in the dream was less than triumphal. But at least I had made myself understood. And as we continued on, I needed to. By the time we reached the beach resort town of Vieste, my condition worsened just as my Italian-speaking fantasies improved. Officially, it wasn't strictly necessary to speak Italian in Vieste because many places were bilingual. Unfortunately for me, the second language was German.

"*Wie geht's?*" the bell captain at the hotel asked helpfully when I had a coughing spell.

By my second day there, things had reached a climax. My symptoms had escalated and so had my fever-induced confidence that I could explain my situation better in Italian then in English. So, armed with several phrases of gibberish I had constructed from my pocket dictionary, I took myself to the nearest pharmacy ready to cut loose. When my turn arrived, I planted myself in front of the kindly-looking pharmacist and let fly. My phrase-book explanations were accompanied by grimaces, frowns, fake coughs, chest-thumping and brow-wiping. My bravura performance had used more body parts than Sophia Loren could have dreamed of and included, of course, a dazzling display of speaking in hands.

When the pharmacist began handing me medicines for cough, fever, ear ache and body pain, I felt a sudden euphoria. She had understood! I was really speaking Italian at last.

Then, without raising so much as a finger, she spoke. "If you have any questions about the medicines, or any further symptoms, please come back," she said. In perfect English.

Mamma Mia

Annelize Goedbloed

*S*unbathing in the scorching heat, a bright green lizard clings to a slit of the whitewashed wall. It slithers away when the woman passes by, dragging plastic bags filled with groceries, sweat beads on her forehead, breathing heavily. She pushes the strings of the fly curtain aside and enters the *trullo* in Alberobello next to mine. I wonder, *Why is it that a wife doesn't seem complete without a plastic bag with food for the family hanging from her arm?*

The nervous jingle of church bells announces it is midday. Lunch time for the family! Soon I hear the rattle of kitchenware next door and Papa arrives calling out:

"*Mina! Sono a casa. Che cosa c'é da mangiare?*" (I am home. What are we eating?)

In Italy a full meal is expected twice a day. *Mamma mia!* I am still digesting last night's dinner: an uncountable number of *antipasti*, then a *primo* of pasta, then a *secondo* of meat, the *contornos* (side courses) of course, then the *dolce* (desert) and then and then . . . . These never-ending delicious meals twice a day are too much for me.

A heavy-set, short, elderly woman with a strong face, an ample bosom and an even more ample waistline, Mina is the typical Italian Mamma presented in Dutch TV commercials where she serves her sumptuous pasta to the large family gathered around a table in a sunny garden. The secret obviously is the advertised brand of Italian olive oil and its best cook: the Italian Mamma!

My temporary neighbor Mina fits the image of seemingly unconditional care for her family and especially its male members. The Italian Mamma is said to leave the toilet seat up for her men after she leaves the bathroom. She reputedly oversees her daughter-in-law's care of her son, so when a girl marries she also marries her mother-in-law. And *she* is the cause of the serious problem of the *bamboccioni* (big babies) or *mammoni* (Mamma's boys), those men who are excessively attached to their Mammas. Indeed, the Italian Mamma is a phenomenon: she is the dutiful cook, caretaker and all-powerful center of the family.

Dino, who manages our rented *trulli* in Alberobello, laughs at my remark. "Yes, exactly my Mamma," he says.

"And the *mammoni*"? I ask.

"A big problem," he confirms, "but the real problem lies with

Mamma. She just loves her son too much and doesn't let him grow into a man and doesn't want him to be independent." But Dino continues to describe his mother lovingly as his *faro*, his lighthouse. *Mamma mia!*

Italy as a country is said to be in a state of emergency. Its very survival is under threat. Italy's birthrate is the second lowest in Western Europe. There are not enough children to support healthy population growth and to match the growing number of elderly. Statisticians and demographers report that more than eighty percent of Italian men well into their thirties still live at home with their parents. There is no rush to get married. Why should they? Mamma takes good care of them; she does their laundry and has their favorite food waiting on the table when they come home. Young men save a lot of money in rental payments, which they spend on cars, electronic gadgets and dating.

The Pope seems as perplexed by the situation as the government. In 2006, he begged Italians to "rediscover the culture of life and love and their mission as parents." Italians, representing one of the most solidly Catholic countries in Europe, ignored his plea to have more children, just as they ignore his teaching on the sinfulness of contraception.

"Italians," one demographer said, "have not given up sex. They have merely given up procreation."

Hoping to confront this national crisis, the Italian Economics Minister is luring Mamma's boys away from home by offering a tax cut for men who leave home and rent their own apartments.

"We must send those we call *bamboccioni* out of the house," the Minister decreed.

The Government has also tried to encourage couples to have babies. Silvio Berlusconi's administration offered money—one thousand Euros—to every woman who gave birth for the first time.

"A ridiculous sum," says Rosaria of Puglia. "If it were a monthly sum for child support like you have in France for example, yes, then it would help." Rosaria is petite, somewhat on the chubby side—the typical Mediterranean woman. She dresses with careful nonchalance, according to the latest orders of Italian fashion designers for colors, décolleté, cut of trousers and beaded sandals. She works in the tourist business and she can hold her job thanks to the help of her mother. *Mamma mia!* The Italian Mammas are the economic lungs of the family.

"But money is not the only thing," she continues. "The mentality has to change in this country. When I was pregnant, I told my boss that I was going abroad for a course, for fear of losing my job. There is the mortgage to pay." She tells me that her husband never learned to do any household chores, but that she is trying to train him. She doesn't consider a second child under the circumstances. "It is hard work to combine a job with a family," she concludes.

A recent study and my informal conversations show that the more the husband is involved in childcare and household chores, the more likely his wife is to want and have a second baby. Italian men do little around the house—fewer than 6 percent of mothers responded that their husbands "always" or "often" did household chores. Consequently, many women cannot face the dual burden of going out to work and looking after a second child, even with the assistance of Mamma.

When sweet, polite Francesco serves me a perfect cappuccino, I grab the chance to talk a little. When I ask him if he lives at home with his mother, he confirms this. He tells me he went north to study so he knows how to live by himself. He is twenty-nine and earns too little to be able to afford a place for himself for the time being, but he is eager to do so. He also tells me that his father does indeed help his mother and does some housework when he comes home. "Papa buys and pours the wine!" Francesco smiles happily.

In Puglia, the ultimate congratulatory wish to the bride is to have a baby boy. While more Italian women are making careers and scoring belated victories for feminism, they paradoxically also—as Mammas—are still doting on their male offspring in the way they always have. Not surprising then that many Italian men believe they are by far the most interesting tourist attraction in the entire country. The reason is simple: their mothers tell them so.

Is the growing equality outside the family really matched by the same tendency inside it? Don't the Italian men still want their wives to look after them as their mothers did? Do they not revel in the role of *bamboccioni*?

On the other hand, because they are so close to Mamma, Italian men are family-oriented and love children. But, above all, they adore women. Is that not wonderful?

On my last day I am happily surprised with my cab driver, a beautiful Italian male. An Italian man flirts like other men breathe: regularly and naturally. And they don't mind my age, because I could be their Mamma. They do adore their Mamma, don't they?

In broken English and Italian, Giuseppe and I engaged in a long conversation. While driving past a good number of the fifty million olive trees of Puglia, he talked about his personal life, views and expectations. He lives with his parents. His father is the official boss but his mother has the real power. They both work and father and mother share household tasks: Papa helps with cleaning but Mamma always cooks. Why should he leave and live on his own? Alone? He likes his family and he loves his mother, so everything is all right.

"Love for Mamma is special," he says. "In the south we are Latin, you know. Latin is in between east and west. We are passionate. We are family men. But I personally am scared to start a family. Emancipation is good. It is good for women to study and work, but a man should always be the boss. And respected. Things have gotten out of hand. My sister, for example: I think she is impossible for a man to live with; she is too emancipated. No respect."

"What do you mean by 'emancipated'?" I ask.

"Women have become too free: they flirt, they do what they want. I am scared because I see and hear what happens with my friends and their wives and girlfriends. There is lots of *tradimento* (treason)," he says vehemently, "No loyalty. We are in between Arabs and European, you see. We don't accept *tradimento*. I don't accept *tradimento*."

I asked if he would be faithful himself.

"Men and women are different," he says, "but I would never leave my wife when she respects me."

"And is it true that the population of Puglia is decreasing?" I ask.

"Yes, I think so. Young people leave, hardly any babies. That is very stupid, because the quality of life in Puglia is good. It is a *capriccio* to go north, earn perhaps a bit more but spend so much more on rent and food that you end up with less money. Prices in Bari are the lowest for Italy, you know. And your family is far away."

We pass the outskirts of Bari. The town is bursting with high-rise concrete apartment towers and industrial developments. The sea glimmers beyond.

Then he says, "Life is good in Puglia."

"Thank you Giuseppe," I respond. "I can see and feel that everywhere."

The cool of the evening revives the town. Terraces around the piazza fill up. Men proudly push prams. A large family has descended on the table next to mine. Isn't life, after all, best spent around a big table eating and chatting, sharing happy moments with those who brought you into the world? A very chubby grandma heaves her bosom over the table to spoon food onto the plates of her children: the grown-ups and the grandchildren. *Viva Mamma Mia!*

THE CASTEL DEL MONTE CONUNDRUM

ROGER NICHOLAS WEBSTER

"*It is more mysterious than you could ever know,*" *said the feeble old man with eyes both crossed and spinning. He startled me as I stood in a small shop of Roman antiquities. His eyes were framed with wrinkles like the rings of a tree. Silver-metallic perspiration glistened on his deeply tanned skin. When he moved his head I noticed he was wearing a dirty yellow yarmulke with an odd zigzag turquoise border.*

"*At night, there are lighted objects flying in and out of the center and beams shining out of each tower,*" *he breathed.*

Suddenly, whoosh! A tall, powerful woman appeared out of nowhere. Seemingly ageless, she was dressed in a grey tailored blouse with epaulets, each bearing a gold embroidered lightening bolt. A thick black leather belt set off a full darker gray skirt. She completely engulfed the man in a bright green cape that was tied around her neck.

With the power of a bullhorn, in a husky voice she cried out, "Pay him no mind, he is crazy!"

She spirited him swiftly out of the shop. The cape with the two of them inside, now turning the color of fire, abruptly started rising. It flattened like a pancake and began to spin. I watched until they disappeared into the dusky evening sky, heading toward a full moon.

I was left alone—all six feet of me feeling tiny and insignificant, but mostly astonished. They spoke perfect English.

"Ring! Ring!" I awoke with a start and answered the phone. I was in a hotel room in Bari, Italy. The concierge was calling to tell me that my luggage was still lost. I sat up, disoriented, remembering the feeling of minuteness and then the fantastic dream. There were travel books scattered on the bed next to me. I'd been reading Stefania Mola's *Castel Del Monte*. I was scheduled to join a writers' tour of Puglia and this fascinating castle was on the itinerary. I was getting the sense that it held secrets beyond understanding.

"A monumental octagonal block, provided with as many towers of the same shape at its corners," Mola writes. And later, "The building is one of the highest expressions of cosmic symbolism involving countless astronomical, geographical, mathematical and geometric connections."

The experts do not agree on when the structure was built, why or by whom. The reigning consensus is that Frederick II had it built in 1240. He was a thirteenth century demigod who during his life acquired the titles King of Germany, Italy, Burgundy,

Sicily, Cyprus, Jerusalem and Holy Roman Emperor. Yet, there is little evidence that Frederick ever slept there. The Castel is not built for habitation, nor does it have a military purpose. One document suggests that the building existed long before Frederick's time. Clearly, here was an ambiguity reminiscent of the Great Pyramid of Giza and the Sphinx of Egypt.

Frederick II was as fascinating as the Castel attributed to him. He was a brilliant egomaniac who believed himself the reincarnation of Christ. He gathered the leading architects, mathematicians, musicians and astrologers of his time to his court. Fibonacci, the great Italian mathematician who introduced Indo-Arabic numerals to the West, was among them. Did this mathematical genius influence the building of the Castel in any way? It has been called a "book of stone," holding the most sophisticated scientific knowledge of the Middle Ages.

At last came the day my group was scheduled to visit the Castel Del Monte. After my dream and advance reading, I was passionate to explore the place.

From the bus window, I stared at the passing landscape. The road was lined with oleander trees in full bloom: pink, white and red. We were about fifteen minutes outside of Andria heading east some thirty miles from the Adriatic coast. The countryside was rough and rocky but beautiful in its sparseness. Miles and miles rolled by. Suddenly, there it was—high on the only hill in sight, surrounded by virtually nothing but acre after acre of stones and sparsely planted trees. It was magnificent and imposing. My anticipation was mounting.

"Unfortunately, we are behind schedule," our Italian guide Marilù announced into the microphone from the front of the bus. "We will only have a half hour in the Castel."

I couldn't believe it. I was irritated, to say the least. The time constraint seemed unreasonable.

We pulled into a large parking lot with a puny tourist shop and coffee bar. A dozen people sat waiting on plastic chairs. The vacant looks on their faces were almost spooky. *It must be the heat*, I thought, as I wiped the sweat from my brow. Screaming cicadas filled the air with an ominous monotony. I paced back and forth as we waited, a clock ticking in my head. At last a second bus appeared to take us to the Castel itself.

I found myself sitting next to a pretty woman in her forties. Curiously, she was reading the same Stefania Mola book that had sent my subconscious into the supernatural a few days before. To break the ice, I laughingly told her about my dream. Her name was Marilyn, and she was a storehouse of information.

"Frederick could have hidden the secrets of the Holy Grail in the architecture," she said. "He was in Palestine during the Crusades. One of his wives was Yolande, Princess of Jerusalem. The Knights Templar there were in contact with Sufi mystics, who honored the God of the three Middle Eastern religions, as did Frederick. He was Christian but was raised with Jews and Muslims in Palermo. The Sufis told the Templars that the Grail had to be placed in a palace in the shape of an octagonal goblet because Jerusalem was an octagonal shaped town."

"Then again, it could have been just a geometrically pleasing hunting lodge; he was a famous falconer," I countered.

"Yes, but the symbol of resurrection is an octagon," she shot back. "It is the shape of imperial sovereignty: the Tower of the Winds in Athens, the Dome of the Rock, Charlemagne's Palatine Chapel in Aachen, San Vitale Basilica in Ravenna. And there are others."

Within five minutes, we were there. Castel del Monte stood eighty feet tall—a beautiful, clean, white limestone edifice surrounded by three perfect concentric circles: one of stone, one of cement and one of pine trees. The vista was awesome. Tiny chamomile flowers filled the cracks in the gently sloping stone steps leading to the door.

"I feel this is a portal into the fairy world," Marilyn said. "There are paranormal vibrations. Nothing was ever built nearby because the energy field won't allow it."

I looked at her intently as we climbed one of the two symmetrical staircases at the entrance. Stone lions stood guard. We entered into the first room and bought tickets.

"Once blind, now we see," she said cryptically, as our eyes adjusted to the darker interior.

"Do you feel the perfection of the measurements?" I asked.

"The room is a trapezoid with the proportions of the Divine Ratio: one to one point six one eight. It's a mystical ratio that shows up everywhere in nature and art. The Great Pyramid was built with it," Marilyn answered.

"Do you remember how important that ratio was to the plot of *The Da Vinci Code?*" I added, glad to be able to contribute something myself.

There are eight rooms on the first floor, all trapezoids with the same proportions. The air is cool; the smell clean but slightly damp. The interior may have once been sumptuous and colorful but is now very plain, mostly white or rose-colored limestone with some window and doorframes made in a brick red conglomerate.

Off the second room, a portal led us into the central courtyard. Here was the pièce de résistance. The top is completely open to clear blue sky, like a giant aperture and again, a perfect octagon. I plunked myself down on the stone floor to take photographs. I really could imagine flying saucers landing here. It was right out of Jules Verne.

"An octagonal shaped fountain was once in the middle. Legend has it that the Castel's architect was drowned in it." Marilyn poured out information. "On the spring and winter solstices, the shadows form a rectangle. The angle of a shadow in the courtyard is forty-seven degrees exactly the same as the Earth's axis."

I looked at my Blackberry; time was moving fast. We flew through the remaining rooms of the ground floor. In the last, were the bones of a grand fireplace and remnants of the ancient mosaic floor, repeating a pattern of six pointed stars in white marble and black slate.

Marilyn was about to expound on this, when Marilù entered the room. She pointed out the famously sophisticated bathroom in one corner, a stairway to the second floor and a roof terrace in another.

"Sorry to say, there is no time to go to the upper floors," Marilù declared. "We are all meeting out front in five minutes."

Marilyn whispered in my ear, "Quick! Come on! There's a better staircase in the fourth room."

We sped from room eight to room seven to the courtyard and into room four. Amazing—there was a definite sequence in getting from one room to another, as if designed for a ceremony of initiation. I imagined initiates going though a succession of transformations as they passed from room to room.

We entered the top floor by a long, tightly winding staircase. The rooms have the same trapezoidal shape and proportions but these all flowed directly from one to another. They were more splendid than the rooms below. Each had ledges along the periphery that could have served as seating for as many as fifty people. Windows to the courtyard were set with seats that looked like thrones. The acoustics were terrific. A speaker, music or chanting would be absolutely hypnotic.

"What on earth happened up here?" I mused.

But there was no time to ponder the mysteries of the upper floor. Out the window, I could see the members of my group were gathered in the front. Obviously, they were waiting for me. I had to go and had only scratched the surface of the puzzles of Castel del Monte.

"Well, it's too unfathomable for me, but maybe I could pitch a screenplay for a *Close Encounters of the Third Kind—Italian Style,* I joked while saying goodbye to Marilyn.

She smiled and asked for a quick hug. I happily complied and only then did I notice that tattooed on her neck, behind her ears, were small neon green lightening bolts.

RUNNING IN PUGLIA

MARY JEAN PRAMIK

*A*n hour before sunrise on a June morning, Puglia beckoned. Stepping out into the dark, the blackened narrow meandering streets of Alberobello opened like a labyrinth before my *trullo*. I was determined to maintain my marathon training schedule. Often when traveling, my resolve to keep up my running fast dilutes with the local wines from the previous nights. But not this trip. Over the years, running for me has become a communication with myself and the earth. Here in Puglia, it became a ritual, like making love to the land at the break of day.

Puglia, the district of southern Italy that fills the rugged heel of the boot-shaped country, stands as the heartland where Mussolini harvested his idea of growing food for the entire country that had become Italy. He intended to create a 'bread basket' for the people. Puglia, an impoverished area far from the fashion centers of northern Italy and five hours away by train from the power seat of Rome, responded. The province now produces tasty durum wheat for semolina, olives and olive oil, vibrant full red wines and a cornucopia of vegetables and fruits.

Without a map or a GPS device, I turned to follow the road out of Alberobello. Named after two feudal wars, *alberobello* means tree of war. The town nestles alongside a riverbed on two sloping hills about an hours' drive from the Adriatic port of Bari. The eastern hill houses the modern area of town, while the western hill hosts the *trulli*, thick-walled houses with conical roofs sometimes marked by white-painted zodiac and religious symbols. Clustered in two neighborhoods—*Rione Monti* and *Rione Aia Piccola*—both boast National Monument status and UNESCO World Heritage site designation.

On Alberobello's Via Don Francesco Gigante, I paced past an austere camping ground. No frills for three euros a night. Scattered hay lay under the automobiles and campers. As I ran up past Via Pasteur, in the early morning mist an elderly man tended geraniums on his balcony, pinching the decaying blossoms, moving slowly from plant to plant.

At the trident crossroads, I turned left on intuition, toward the spreading rays cresting on the horizon. I recalled a friend asking on a recent evening, "When will you stop this lifestyle?" He meant the repetitive hours of training required each day to achieve a level of fitness for some unnamed event. I had not thought of it as a lifestyle.

"I don't do lifestyles," I told him. "I try to live a life."

Thrusting again toward the horizon, I recalled the Academy Award winning 1981 British film *Chariots of Fire*. I heard its soaring Vangelis synthesizer score as each foot struck the paved country lane. In the film, the Scottish track phenom Eric Liddell raced over the moors above the sea. In one scene, his sister Jennie worried that her brother's interest in running and training for the 1924 Summer Olympics distracted him from their work as missionaries in China.

Reflecting on his sister's concerns, Liddell commented on his running "I believe that God made me for a purpose . . . [the mission in China], but He also made me fast, and when I run, I feel His pleasure." Though I am not religious, I understand Liddell's sentiment.

Through sports training, I first explored my physical self because my body was my most immediate contact with the earth. I reasoned that my current form is the only body housing my mind and any creative spirit available in this lifetime.

At the end of any race, I experience a curious kick during the last fifty meters. My body grinds into hyperspeed as I focus on the finish line. There is a joy in this movement I had not previously experienced in my life. My legs turn over faster, I angle toward the finish. No matter how exhausted I felt seconds before, my entire being springs forward and zooms. Zipping over the responsive blacktop paved road leading out of Alberobello in the cool

morning, I understand the sense of Eric Liddell's feeling the deity's pleasure in running. Fast I may not be, but the first light cresting over the eastern horizon lifted my feet and tightly-fitted worn running shoes.

In this rock-strewn rough heel of the land that is Puglia, the Italian earth is red, rich as if it absorbed the blood of ancient Messapians, Greeks, Carthaginians and Romans. As the light began to open the sky, I avoided a black-spotted pale green lizard on the sidewalk. I followed the rising sun past home gardens with tall tomato bushes, zucchini blooming golden yellow, each plot hosting several olive and fig trees. Humming birds darted in and out of the blossoms as I passed.

Gliding by the garden center on my left, I inhaled the clay essence of the various shaped terra cotta pots upended one on top the other, waiting for homes later in the day. Then, I took leave of what resembled a town. Now running at a brisk pace up, each step took me further out into farm lands past cherry trees pregnant with bright red orbs that perked up like nipples on a breast. Blurring past were the gray stone *trulli* where farmers housed the tools of their trade or stored hay for animals nearby.

The amaranthine earth, redolent with iron and assorted minerals, pulled me toward it with a sensuous primordial beckoning. Chicory caressed the stone fences that lined the road. I could feel the sea in this land residing between the Adriatic and the Ionian Seas.

At a "Y" in the road, I first followed the orange arrow identifying *Regione Puglia* and *Bosco Selva Comunale* and *Silva Arboris Belli*. With rudimentary Italian and Latin roots from high school, running during these hours did not require a dictionary. I aimed toward the community forest, the beautiful trees. Pine and a touch of balsa scented the gentle zephyr that meandered through the needles. The morning air cleared my breathing, allowing for a faster pace. Yet another horizontal stone fence bordered the forest of curving trees. Along the roadside, a camper stood in quiet contemplation.

I retraced my course and headed to the right at the "Y" in the direction of the *Az Agricola del Trulli* arrow. More *trulli* hid slightly behind higher flat-stoned fences. In one grove of gray-barked olives, a pyre quietly burned with the smoke snaking along the red soil into the dawn as an unseen Puglian cleared his orchard of debris. A crimson-painted wrought-iron gate stood slightly ajar between stone fences, an open invitation. As the sun rose, the inhabitants began to stir out into their fields, checking tomatoes, onions, artichokes. A lone man in blue pants and white shirt and cap watered his blooming green peppers neatly ordered in five long rows. Through the leafy branches of cherry trees that bordered his plot, I watched as he stooped over to tenderly prune each plant, much like my father had done so frequently through his ninety-one years. Watching this farmer flooded me with memories of so many Ohio summer mornings when my father would tend his garden before leaving for work in the coal mines.

The gnarled olives and figs extended their branches as I ran toward them, welcoming me. I retraced the roads and crossings back towards Alberobello. Small tractor-like vehicles began to pass slowly. The drivers nodded. Passing a furry-blossomed tree nearing town, thousands of bees swirled about and dove at the white flowers.

I ran through Piazza Curri past the Basilica de SS Medici down the hill in the new town, past the glorious Cantina restaurant where some nights friends and I feasted on succulent *buratta*—ricotta wrapped in fresh mozzarella, a vibrant house wine, and two exquisite desserts, sugar from the last entry powering my run this morning. Stepping lightly so as not to awaken the inhabitants, I tripped past Piazza Mario Pagano, a former threshing center in the town where farmers brought their harvested wheat and other grains to contribute their required allotment to the local count's stores.

For ten mornings during these running meditations, I fell in love with Puglia, a land offering a verdant sustenance for body and soul alike.

STONES UNTURNED

CAROL J. KELLY

On a sunny afternoon in Lecce's Piazzetta Falconieri, I started to warm up to stones. I had already been in Puglia for a few days and admired the centuries-old baroque architecture and decorative stonework in every square and on most streets and alleyways. But stones generally leave me cold, despite their stoic beauty.

As Marilù, our Italian tour guide, proudly pointed out the soft, pinkish, local limestone, I touched a nearby portico and felt the powdery residue on my fingers. And in that moment, something shifted. I got it. Puglia's easy-to-carve *pietra gentila* or *pietra leccese* limestone made possible the region's elaborately beautiful buildings, especially its cathedrals and basilicas. Lecce was the heart of it all—the very center from which an extravagant style of stonework, known as *barocco Leccese*, developed between the sixteenth and the early eighteenth century and spread throughout southern Italy, giving Pugliese towns their distinctive look.

This over-the-top architectural style flourished in the seventeenth century Counter-Reformation era when the church was intent on reasserting its power. Stonework was the cornerstone of the church's campaign to impress and win people back to its pews. Lecce's lavish Basilica di Santa Croce, commissioned in the middle of the sixteenth century by the rich Order of Celestines, is one of the finest examples of the city's baroque style. At first glance, I felt overwhelmed by its overly ornate façade and couldn't figure out the iconography of its three distinct sections. Chrysa, the youngest and sharpest-eyed member of our travel group, helped me to distinguish some richly carved symbolic figures high up above the balcony of the church's main entrance.

"Cherubs show the happy face of religion," Marilù said, "and back then, most people couldn't read, so images were important." I understood why these lavish friezes and stone carvings inspired awe. And it made sense that the dramatic church and adjoining convent buildings, now the seat of the local government, were as Marilù said, "conceived like a theatre."

From Lecce, the "rock star" of stonework, to the humble, unadorned *trulli* of Alberobello, stones silently tell the story of Puglia's past. It's a tale of serfdom and poverty as well as wealth and power. Italians etch and build their lives in stone. Frederick II, King of Sicily and Holy Roman Emperor, contributed forty stone castles to the region's landscape—the most impressive being Castel del Monte, built in 1240 on a hilltop in Andria. The Romans used interlocking stones to build Via Appia, the first superhighway and the tactical route to much of Italy's history. In Oria's La Basilica Cattedrale, stones wore makeup—stucco walls were painted to look like marble. In Matera, peasants lived inside stone caves, or *sassi*, for centuries. And limestone *grotte* (caves) revealed Puglia's subterranean world, exhibiting natural "rock art," formed by stalactites and stalagmites. Simple stone fences that looked like ribbons in the fields were a fixture on *masserie* (farms). Stones were everywhere. The way they were used revealed the infrastructure, culture, economics, art and history of the south. Stones underpin Puglia's cultural identity—contributing much more than building blocks for the region's architectural gems.

In Oria, I was fooled. Basilica Cattedrale's brightly colored rococo interior was impressive, and while I thought I was looking at real marble walls, they were expertly painted stucco. "There are no quarries of colored marble in our region so it was very expensive to import marble from other regions," said Prof. Pino Malva, the author of tourist guidebook, *I Colori di Oria* (The Colors of Oria), and our host as we toured his vibrant city. "So in order to save money, they thought to decorate the walls in that way."

In an email later, Prof. Malva had more to say about the "fake" marble, "Really because of historical and economic reasons, the cathedral's walls remained white for much time and the decoration was completed only in 1912, according to the ancient plans. The colored stucco is also called 'Venetian Stucco' because in the eighteenth century it was used very much in that wonderful city."

Sandstone, Prof. Malva added, was used to build the outside of the cathedral while limestone was used only for the decorations of doors, dripstones and the Corinthian capitals because it was easier to carve. "Sandstone is a typical stone of Salento," he said, "and much more rugged than limestone."

There are two kinds of sandstone, Prof. Malva continued: "The first kind, called tufo, tender and white, is used for building the walls of common houses; the second kind, called *carparo*, hard and colored [yellow or brown] is used for important buildings." He said *carparo* changes color according to the position of the sun. "In fact, in the morning it seems to be brown, in the afternoon it seems to be yellow and at the sunset it appears pink-red colored, and this gives to the front wall of the cathedral a particular charm."

Later that afternoon, Prof. Malva led our travel group up a hill to Castello Suevo, built by Frederick II between 1227 and 1233, mostly using hard, local sandstone that looked yellow in the hot sun. As I walked to the roof and got great views of Oria and surrounding Pugliese towns, I thought: the oldest stones of this castle had weathered almost eight hundred years!

In Alberobello, the home base of our travel group, more than a thousand exquisite cone-roofed *trulli* told a rags-to-riches tale. Overlapping limestone slabs were literally the roofs over heads of poor farmers and their lifestock; now *trulli* have become sought-after property for resort developers and foreign investors. *Trulli* were built without mortar so, in feudal times, the stones could quickly be disassembled into a pile when the tax collector came.

I had the distinct pleasure of living in a *trullo* loft apartment on Via Monte Sabotino for almost two weeks. The comfortable, renovated space that I shared with my roommate, Nancy, stayed nice and cool even when temperatures soared above 90°F. The high ceiling gave our apartment an airy feel, despite the small, narrow windows, while its thick limestone walls and stacked-stone roof functioned like ancient air-conditioning. When I wanted to feel *soleone* (lion sun, or the hottest sun of the summer) and catch a lovely breeze, I sat on the limestone steps in front of our *trullo* and watched locals and tourists walk by.

The simple, unfussy design of *trulli*—many dating back to the fifteenth century—contrasted starkly with Lecce's baroque architecture. But the stones used to build them served their purpose: varying degrees of form and function. For me, Alberobello's modern *trullo* church, Chiesa Sant'Antonio (completed in 1927), with its gigantic, central, cone-shaped dome, or cupula, was more approachable than Basilica Cattedrale. I enjoyed a quiet moment in the updated *trullo* church, appreciating its stone interior.

Matera, in neighboring Basilicata, was magical. Standing at the top of a hill looking down at the sprawling cave city set at the

rim of a deep ravine, I could imagine what it would be like to wake up in the eighth century—stoned! The ravine gave me a glimpse of the dry, rocky limestone in the Murgia bedrock, the geological foundation of the region. Its fertile limestone plateau between the Adriatic and Ionian coasts has been cultivated by generations of farmers, starting with the Messapians. People have lived in these cave dwellings, or *sassi*, for two millennia—since the Palaeolithic Age.

Along with my travel companions, I visited Casa Grotta, a typical *sasso* in Vico Solitario, and was amazed that ancient peasants shared their tiny caves with livestock. Chickens lived under the very high bed and the back of the cave had a "stable" for the family's horse, and even sheep and pigs. The tufa interior was whitewashed—I had a feeling this had to be done often.

That Matera's *sassi* and Alberobello's *trulli* have been designated UNESCO World Heritage Sites highlights the importance of the south's stone dwellings not only to Italian culture but to world culture. These stones preserve valuable history for future generations everywhere. And Italy has more World Heritage Sites than any other country in Europe.

In the town of Castro on the Adriatic coast, I saw different types of limestone caves on a trip to the prehistoric Grotta Zinzulusa. It was a hot, sunny day but the caves were chilly, damp and uncomfortable. The thin stalactites had an eerie quality to them and I was bored while our group waited in an endless queue to enter the cave. It was worth the wait. I got a better sense of the importance of Italy's longest, natural subterranean network, Puglia's rocky coastline, its limestone plateau, prehistoric sea caves and the unique ecosystem that has nurtured a highly diverse mix of plants and animals, including unique sponges. As well, the cave is home to fossil remains of birds, bovines, felines, deer, horses, rhinoceroses, elephants, bears, hippopotamuses and Neolithic and Eneolithic earthenware. Fossils etch history in stone.

On my last evening in Italy, I was strolling the narrow stone streets of Bari's old town (a summer *passeggiata*, or evening stroll, was easy to adopt) when I came upon a roped-off, carefully pre-served, old section of Roman road in Piazza del Ferrarese. I observed two levels—on top were large, squared paving stones in a fairly regular arrangement, all similar in size and shape, while below were smaller slabs of random shapes, laid irregularly. The Romans used volcanic ash to cement the stones. Porta Nuova, as it was labeled, seemed like a side view or an "MRI cross-section" of a sophisticated highway-construction technique used to build Via Appia connecting Rome to Brindisi—a project that was begun in 312 BCE. When completed, the Appian Way covered about three hundred and sixty miles. It was the first superhigh-way.

At sunset, as I came to terms with the waning moments of my trip, I sat on the stone steps of Cattedrale San Sabino in Bari's old city watching families and groups of friends walk about the piazza. The steps were warm, holding the heat of the day's sun. I glanced wistfully at the cathedral's stone façade, which had recently been cleaned and looked creamy and pure in the sun's yellow-orange glow. In the distance, mostly hidden by the buildings in the piazza, Castello Svevo's thick sandstone looked yellow in the dimming light. The slightly decrepit castle was first a Roman fort, then was incorporated by the Byzantines in the eleventh century before the Normans had their turn. The sprawling castle suited its ordinary coastal setting in Bari; it couldn't compete with the imposing, octagonal Castel del Monte (also called the Crown of Stone) or with Puglia's many other impressive castles.

I started to think of stones as a gift from nature to Puglia's artists and architects. Of course, it was a much more generous gift as these stones have graced world history and culture. I was stuck on stones. Perhaps Frederick II was on to something—he knew imperial stone castles would be his timeless legacy.

Magna Graecia

Barbara J. Euser

"Acquire land and found a city where you see rain falling from a clear sky," the Oracle at Delphi had pronounced. What kind of instructions were those? How could Phalanthos lead a group of colonists all the way across the sea to that far peninsula with only that to go on?

Other aspiring Greek colonists had been given better directions. Following the famine twenty-six years before, the Chalcidians, for example, had received instructions to found their city at the mouth of the Apia River. That was a place one could look for. And by all accounts, Rhegion was now a flourishing city in Calabria.

Besides, Phalanthos had heard that Sikonyia was a desirable location. He could happily take his followers there. He would go back and ask for a blessing to settle somewhere he had at least heard of. Accompanied by Partheniai, his best friend from Sparta, Phalanthos returned to the Oracle.

The Oracle replied, "Fair is the land between Corinth and Sikyon, but you will not settle there. Look to Satyrion, the water of Taras, a harbor to the left, and the place where the goat loves salt water, wetting the tip of his grey beard. There build Taras."

The Oracle rarely gave the answer one wanted to one's questions. All right then, he would not go to Sikonyia, he would follow the edge of the narrow peninsula until he passed Satyrion and would find the next best harbor. Satyrion had been established about the same time as Rhegion. As far as he had heard, the local inhabitants had tolerated the new settlers. But Phalanthos would take no unnecessary chances. He would find a location that could be defended from attack.

ᎲᎬ

The winds had been fair all the way from Arcadia. The voyagers had been at sea for four days, out of sight of land for the last two.

The coast of Puglia appeared first as a vague blue line on the horizon, barely distinguishable from the sea. As the voyagers watched, hour after hour, the line grew firm, details appeared. The coast varied from imposing stone cliffs, to hills, to flat terrain. But Phalanthos sailed on, searching for the ideal landing. Following the coastline as it turned north, he continued on until they came to a large bay. At the inner edge of the bay he found a narrow entrance into a small secluded harbor. There he dropped anchor. On this spit of land he would found the city the Oracle had named Taras.

❧

The year was 706 BCE. The voyagers were Spartans, sent as colonists from their mother-city, their *metropolis*. The colonists were seeking a land of opportunity; Sparta was seeking a connection for commerce and trade. The colonists had brought with them some of the sacred fire from the public hearth in Sparta. They would use it to kindle the public hearth of their new settlement. Taras would maintain its connection to its mother city for centuries, regularly sending gifts and representatives back to Sparta. When Taras grew strong enough to send out its own colonists, it consulted Sparta in advance.

The colonists found a hospitable countryside, land that was stony but fertile, surrounded by the bounteous sea. They cleared the stones from the fields, using them to build stone fences that stretched for miles. They planted roots of olive trees and grapevines they had carried with them from home. They buried their dead in a necropolis outside the city walls. As Taras grew, they built piazzas and temples in the style of Arcadia. Two Doric columns of the Temple of Poseidon still grace the waterfront of Taras, Rome's Tarentum, today's Taranto.

Meanwhile, other Greek city-states were sending out their own colonists to establish outposts on the shores of the Italian peninsula. More than thirty city-states established multiple colonies, spread from the southern coast of the Iberian peninsula (today's Spain) to the shores of the Black Sea (today's Turkey). Important Greek colonies in today's Italy were Rhegion, established by Chalcis; Syracuse, by Corinth; Cyme, by Aeolis; Ischia and Cuma (near Naples) by Chalcis; and Elea (Velia) in Campania by Phocaea. Other Greek colonies included Naples, Akragas, Subaris, Locri, Cortone, Turii, Gallipoli and Ancona. Magna Grecia, as the region was called, spread from Sicily through the south of the boot-shaped peninsula, from Calabria on the tip of the boot, to Puglia, its high heel.

The Greeks established permanent colonies and actively traded throughout the region. Archeologists trace the trading activities of these ancient Greeks by the troves of Greek coins they have uncovered.

The Greeks also brought their alphabet with them. The Chalcidean/Cumaean form of the Greek alphabet was first adopted by the Etruscans, who had arrived in the north of the peninsula about a hundred years before the Greeks arrived in the south. The Etruscan alphabet evolved into the Latin alphabet, the most widely-used alphabet in the world.

Greek colonists in Puglia lived in uneasy proximity with the Messapii, people who had arrived from Illyria (today's Albania) several hundred years before the first Greeks arrived. The

Messapii lived in heavily fortified cities including Manduria and Oria. Though they competed for control of the countryside, the Greeks dominated the Puglian coast, from today's Bari to Otranto to Taranto. At Egnazia, the Greeks overran the Messapii and turned the city into a model sea port. Today, the ruins are a protected archeological site, with a museum of treasures recovered from the graves of both Messapii and Greeks.

Although marred by periodic wars against each other, both cultures flourished side-by-side until the Roman armies descended on the south. The Greeks and Messapii united under King Pyrrhus of Epirus to fight against the enemy from the north. From 280 to 275 BCE, battles raged. But even their combined strength was not enough. Following the Pyrrhic War, both Magna Graecia and Messapia were absorbed into the Roman Empire.

Latin replaced Greek as the language of the learned, sophisticated ruling class. However, the Greek language survived among its subjugated speakers as the language of laborers, used within families at home.

For almost six hundred years, Roman rule was absolute in former Magna Graecia. When Theodosius I died in 395 CE, the Roman Empire was divided between his two sons. The Western Roman Empire was overrun by the Goths in the fourth century, and by the fifth century had disintegrated into a patchwork of warring kingdoms. The Eastern Roman Empire, with its capital in Constantinople, remained intact and strong. Greek replaced Latin as the official language of the Empire, and the Eastern

Roman Empire became known as the Byzantine Empire.

Emperor Justinian I, who ruled from 527-565 CE, reestablished the Empire's control over the south of Italy. His Greek-speaking troops found a sympathetic population of Greek speakers in the former Magna Graecia. Waves of Orthodox Christian Greeks arrived from Greece and the eastern Mediterranean during the Early Middle Ages. They established Greek Orthodox churches and monasteries throughout Puglia. The most important of these monasteries was St. Nicola di Casole in the Salentine region, a monastery, cultural center and school, with a particularly rich library. Manuscripts from the library are now housed in museums including those in Florence, the Vatican City, Paris, London and Berlin.

However, this renaissance of Magna Graecia was once again threatened from the north, first by the Lombards, then by the Normans. Pope Nicolo II wanted to establish Roman Catholic rule over the south and, with the Melfi Agreement of 1059 CE, legitimized the Norman campaign. Although the Normans established the Roman Catholic Church in Puglia, the Greek Orthodox Church survived in certain areas, such as the Salento, for another five hundred years. During the Counter-Reformation in the sixteenth century, Rome officially abolished Greek Orthodox rites.

When the Normans drove out the Byzantine administration, Latin once again replaced Greek as the official language of the region. But the Greek language survived in small pockets, including certain towns around Lecce, in the Salento province.

Today, there are two areas of the former Magna Graecia where Greek is still spoken: in Reggio Calabria, the very tip of the toe of Italy's boot, and in Grecia Salentina in Puglia. Although the dialects have evolved over the centuries, speakers of Grecanico in Calabria can converse with speakers of Griko in Salento. Linguists debate whether today's Griko and Grecanico derive from the original Greek colonists or from the Byzantine Middle Ages. Because many ancient Greek words are found in both dialects, the consensus is that the Greek dialects spoken today descend from the first colonists in the 700s BCE.

The government of Italy has recognized both communities as official linguistic minorities and the European Union has granted Griko status as an endangered language. The result of this official recognition has given Griko-speaking communities the right to use the language in street signs and in radio broadcasts and to teach Griko language and culture in elementary schools.

As the Greek language survived the centuries, so did other aspects of Greek culture, including Greek music. When the Greek Orthodox church was banned, believers sang their Mass in Greek in the streets. Today, during Holy Week, *I Passiuna tu Christù* (Christ's Passion) is performed by two street singers accompanied by an accordion player. Similarly, *La Strina* is a song about the birth and infancy of Christ.

The *taranta*, a popular folk dance of Puglia, was traditionally danced by women who would twirl ecstatically until they collapsed, exhausted. The *taranta* is reputedly descended from the rituals of the cult of Dionysus, the ancient Greek god of wine, in which his followers, the Bacchae, would dance ecstatically until collapse.

The grapevines brought by Greek colonists to Puglia, the genesis of wine itself, have also survived the centuries. Several varietals, now considered native to Puglia, were actually introduced to the peninsula from Greece. According to legend, Aeneas, leading the few survivors of Troy to settle in Italy, carried the *Uva di Troia* (Grapes of Troy) with him. *Negro Amaro* grapes, thriving around the Bay of Taranto, may have been brought to Puglia by Pharanthos himself. *Negro Amaro* grapes are often blended with *Malvasia Nera di Lecce*, *Malvasia* being another variety of grapes that originated in Greece around Monemvasia. *Aglianico*, *Grecanico* and *Greco* varietals were also introduced to Italy by some of the original Greek colonists. For the early colonists, selling wine to Greek colonies in Africa was a lucrative trade. Wine made from these grapes is still lucrative trade in Puglia.

On a recent trip to Puglia, I sat with a friend in a small piazza, drinking a glass of wine from the DOC (Certified Original Location) of Salice Salentino Rosso. The ruby red wine was a *Leverano Vigna Del Saraceno Malvasia*, bottled by the Conti Zecca Estate. We were in the town of Calimera, whose name means "good morning" in Greek. Its whitewashed buildings, baking in the strong sun, looked like any other small town in Puglia, except for its street signs. They were written in Greek—names in Italian appearing on the second line. At a nearby table, two old men conversed in a language that sounded like Greek. The excellent wine was from vines of Greek origin; the language surrounding us was Greek; we were reading signs written in the Greek alphabet. Yes, we were in Puglia. But we were in one of the nine towns of Puglia called the Grecia Salentina, where the heritage of Magna Graecia remains clear.

On an ancient Greek burial stone in a small park in Calimera is the inscription: *Zeni su en ise ettù sti Kalimera* (You are not a stranger here in Calimera). If Phalanthos were here today, he would feel at home.

About the Contributors

NANCY ALPERT grew up in Long Beach and transplanted to the Bay Area, where she received a B.A. in psychology from Stanford University and an M.S.W. from UC Berkeley. She traveled in Europe, Russia, China, Mexico, Tahiti, and lived in Italy and Israel before she finally rooted and blossomed in San Francisco. Of her many accomplishments working with seniors during twenty years as a Family Service Agency social worker, Nancy's proudest was launching the Senior Peer Counseling program, which connected seniors to each other as resources. However, nothing she had done previously rivaled the thrill and satisfaction of her daughter's birth in 2001. When her marriage and job ended almost simultaneously, Nancy re-examined her strengths and interests, paid attention to the dozens of diaries and a poetry award on the shelves, and acknowledged the happiness she'd always felt going to the library. She realized it was now time to take her writing seriously. Nancy has spent the last year or so exploring various writing genres and discovering that the world of children's books especially delights her, excites her—and practically ignites her! When she's not on fire, Nancy enjoys reading, knitting, visiting with family and friends, undergoing shopping therapy and above all else, crafting her very personal story of what it means to be a Mom.

$\mathcal{D}$ENISE ALTOBELLO, daughter of a butcher and a restaurant maven, granddaughter of a German gravedigger and a one-armed Cajun barbeque chef, hails originally from the now famous Ninth Ward of New Orleans, just downriver from the French Quarter. Growing up among the graveyards of her Irish, German and African-American neighbors, she played hide-and-seek in the cities of the dead, learned to decipher the voodoo markings adorning the above-ground graves and honed her skills in palm reading, bar-hopping and fire baton twirling. Her achievements include the title of runner-up as Miss Majorette of Louisiana and a five-year reign as fancy strut champion for the National Baton Twirlers Association. In recent years, her most interesting travel adventures included working (for three days) as an itinerant goat milker and cooking paella in the back of a steamy truck in Provence. A two-year veteran of Writers' Workshops International, Denise authored two stories in *Venturing in Ireland: Quest for the Modern Celtic Soul*. When she is not cooking, eating, drinking or gardening, she teaches English at Trinity Episcopal School in the Lower Garden District of New Orleans.

$\mathcal{J}$OANNA BIGGAR is a teacher, writer and traveler whose special places of the heart include the California coast and the South of France. She has degrees in Chinese and French and, as a professional writer for twenty years, has written poetry, fiction, personal essays, features, news and travel articles for hundreds of publications including *The Washington Post Magazine, Psychology Today, The International Herald Tribune,* and *The Wall Street Journal.* Her book *Travels and Other Poems* was published in 1996, and her most recent travel essays have appeared in *Sportsfanmagazine.com* and *Floating through France: Life Between Locks on the Canal du Midi, Venturing in Southern Greece: The Vatika Odysseys,* and *Venturing in Ireland: Quest for the Modern Celtic Soul.* She has taught journalism, creative writing, personal essay and travel writing at The Writer's Center in Bethesda since 1984, and in recent years has taught reading and writing at St. Martin de Porres Middle School and Emiliano Zapata Street Academy in Oakland, California.

*S*ANDRA BRACKEN made the first of many journeys alone to Peru in 1976 where she walked the hills around Sacsayhuaman, photographed the stonework there and chartered a plane to fly over the lines at Nazca—all in the pursuit of art. More recently, with her husband, travels have been in pursuit of fish. She is an artist by education and sensibility, has a Master's Degree in Fine Arts and taught drawing for twenty years. Her sculpture has been exhibited in galleries and museums in the United States and is in private collections. A chap book of poems, *New Moon,* was published in 1999. She collaborated on *Meet Me at the Wayside Body Shop,* a collection of poems and collages, in 2003. Travel stories were included in *Venturing in Ireland: Quest for the Modern Celtic Soul*, 2007. She lives in Maryland with her husband, near their three children and five grandchildren.

NNELIZE GOEDBLOED is full-bred Dutch and works and lives in Delft, The Netherlands. Born in Indonesia—a Dutch colony at the time—she spent her toddler years as a "guest" of the Emperor of Japan. This implied early exposure to creeping and crawling animal life and inspired her to study parasitology and—as a more hygienic counter balance— marine biology (at Leyden University). While birthing her four children, she needed to be at home and thus started breeding pedigree Texel sheep and special chicken breeds. Annelize's work has always been in the medical field, and she calls herself a medically derailed biologist. She worked in clinical research throughout Europe and in Israel. After having grown quite cynical about the medical trade she founded her own company (BioClin) with her son that specializes in preventive medicinal products. Her writing has been for science (clinical studies, reports, lectures) and therefore predominantly in English—the trade language. She loves travelling and her contribution to *Venturing in Ireland: Quest for the Modern Celtic Soul* were her first efforts in travel writing, which she wants to pursue. With thirteen grandchildren, the family breeding ventures are finished for now.

CONNIE GUTOWSKY was born in The Dalles, Oregon. She graduated from the University of Oregon and from the University of the Pacific McGeorge School of Law. She joined the Sacramento County Public Defender's Office and later went into private practice. She began studying and writing poetry when she retired from the practice of law in 2001. Connie is up early most mornings reading or writing what she calls her homemade bread of poetry in sonnets, triolets, villanelles, sestinas and often free verse—poems which she brings to a writing group every month. Her poems have appeared in *Calaveras Station Literary Journal* and she has a chapbook out, *Autumn's Flush*. She wrote a children's story, *Ronald and Peter Go Camping*. She has an essay in *Venturing in Ireland: Quest for the Modern Celtic Soul*. Connie lives in Sacramento with her husband of forty-six years, Al. She loves her family, books, bridge, naps, friends and mornings.

THOMAS HARRELL has joined the ranks of former lawyers who became writers. After sixteen years working for a Wall Street firm, the last six on dialysis, he received a new kidney five years ago. With this second chance, he decided to leave the law and pursue two of his life passions: travel and writing. He has traveled to numerous countries since then, although not nearly enough yet. He has written about travel in several of these countries, including Argentina, Bosnia, China and Italy. He also writes personal essays, many about his upbringing in the South, and occasionally ventures into poetry. He studied history and politics in college and hopes to write a novel incorporating travel and history. He lives in San Francisco, California.

AROL J. KELLY was born in Jamaica and came to the United States right after high school. She considers herself bicultural, seeing the world through the lens of a small Caribbean island and as a U.S. citizen and longtime New Yorker. After starting out in media research, she changed career paths, becoming the associate editor of a newsmagazine run by a nonprofit organization, written by and for teenagers in New York City's public high schools. She then worked for four newspapers including *The Boston Globe* and *The Wall Steet Journal*, where she's currently an assistant news editor for the Asian and European editions. She has been published in newspapers, but plans to revive her creative writing ambitions with poetry, personal essays and a family memoir. Italy is one of her special places of the heart—she has been besotted since the summer of 1995 when she spent ten blissful days on tour. Carol, who is also passionate about tennis, lives in Brooklyn.

*L*AURIE MCANDISH KING is the daughter of a banker, science teacher, poet, scuba diver and UFO investigator (only two parents, like other earthlings). Laurie McAndish King has chased lemurs through the mountains of Madagascar, studied medicinal plants in the jungles of Brazil, tracked lions in Botswana and trapped raptors in the Marin Headlands. Her award-winning travel essays have been published in anthologies such as *Venturing in Ireland: Quest for the Modern Celtic Soul, 30 Days in Italy, The Thong Also Rises* and *The Kindness of Strangers.* Her work has also been published in the *San Francisco Chronicle Magazine* and aired on KUSF radio. Laurie co-edited, along with Linda Watanabe McFerrin, two volumes of *Hot Flashes: sexy little stories & poems.* She pays the bills as a marketing consultant, podcasts in her spare time, earned her Master's Degree in Internet-based education and publishes an online newsletter for travel writers at *www.travelwritersnews.com.* Laurie indulges her passions for travel, anthropology and natural history as often as she possibly can.

*L*INDA WATANABE MCFERRIN, poet, travel writer, novelist and teacher, is a contributor to numerous journals, newspapers, magazines, anthologies and online publications including the *San Francisco Examiner, The Washington Post, The San Francisco Chronicle Magazine, Modern*

Bride, Travelers' Tales, Salon.com, and *Women.com.* She is the author of two poetry collections and the editor of the 4th edition of *Best Places Northern California.* A winner of the Nimrod International Journal Katherine Anne Porter Prize for Fiction, her work has also appeared in *Wild Places* and *American Fiction.* Her novel, *Namako: Sea Cucumber* was published by Coffee House Press and named Best Book for the Teen-Age by the New York Public Library. Her collection of award-winning short stories, *The Hand of Buddha,* was published in 2000. She is also co-editor of a prize-winning travel anthology and the recently released *Hot Flashes: sexy little stories & poems.* Linda has served as a judge for the San Francisco Literary Awards and the Kiriyama Prize. She holds an undergraduate degree in Comparative Literature and a Master of Arts degree in Creative Writing and is the founder of Left Coast Writers (http://leftcoastwriters.com). When she is not on the road, she directs art, consults on communications.

ETHEL MUSSEN is well into her eighth decade and hardly believing it. Ethel looks back at a half-century career in health care, latterly in speech pathology and audiology. Being the wife of a UC professor offered an incidental life of travel and spawned a family of one daughter, one son, and one spunky grandson. Retirement at seventy gave her freedom to pursue interests in collecting, especially French ceramics from

Moustiers in Provence, with frequent trips to the village. Travel writing was meant to publicize these friends, but classes and networking led to more friendships among travelers and writers and publication in *Travelers' Tales* and *Floating Through France: Life between Locks on the Canal du Midi*. Puglia offered an opportunity to return to Italy where the Mussens had spent a glorious year in 1960-61 (when *Volare* first was sung at San Remo). This 2008 summer was enriched by becoming steeped in medieval history and making the acquaintance of Frederick II—that lovable old wonder of the world—and spending a Hollywoodish day with Al Bano Carrisi—that lovable old winemaker and showman. Further joy came from the warmth of simpatico companions, whose sharp ears heard what hearing aids had blurred, and who graciously corrected inadvertent errors. With or without a masseur's tattoos, everyone helped to provide a truly therapeutic adventure.

MARY JEAN PRAMIK has credentials in medical and science journalism where she mined scientific metaphors and labored to discover alternatives to the passive voice so beloved by scientists and physicians. She is the editor (a.k.a. ghostwriter) of the pharmaceutical thriller *Norethindrone; the First Three Decades* that charts the tortuous development of the first birth control pill and resides in most medical libraries. Ms. Pramik is an award-winning writer in medical advertising and has published in *Nature Biotechnology, Drug*

Topics, and *Cosmetic Surgery News* as well as mainstream publications such as *Good Housekeeping* and the *National Enquirer*. She has contributed to three recent Traveler's Tales anthologies, *Floating Through France: Life between Locks on the Canal du Midi*, *Venturing in Southern Greece: the Vatika Odysseys*, and *Venturing in Ireland: Quest for the Modern Celtic Soul* as well as to *Odyssey Magazine*. Schooled in the biological sciences and literary arts, she taught comparative anatomy at Case Western Reserve University, Cleveland, Ohio, and conducted neuroendocrinology and biophysical research at the University of California San Francisco prior to entering the writing profession. A seasoned resident of the San Francisco Bay Area, Ms. Pramik moonlights as a biotech day laborer, political activist and fledgling triathlete. She is currently at work on an M.F.A. in Writing, a novel entitled *GEM of Egypt*, and a book of essays, *Know It All*, among other endeavors.

ELEANOR SHANNON, a native of Charlottesville, Virginia, has lived most of her adult life in New England (Massachusetts and New Hampshire). An avid traveler, who speaks French and Italian, she has been teaching in an honors program for Italian university students in Milan for the past four years. Previously, she taught business at the University of Virginia, did strategic management consulting in Boston, worked at the World Bank in Washington, D.C. and Africa, and taught

French and Italian in intensive summer programs at Dartmouth College. She also took a significant period out of full-time work to raise three children. Her home is in the Back Bay of Boston.

CHRYSA TSAKOPOULOS is a native of Sacramento, California and recently graduated from Georgetown University's School of Foreign Service with a degree in International History, with the dream of one day becoming a professor. In spring 2007, she spent a college semester studying at the Universita' Cattolica Del Sacro Cuore in Milano. She enjoys travelling, dancing of all types, learning new languages, and has recently fallen in love with the harp. She has contributed essays to the anthologies *Venturing in Southern Greece: The Vatika Odysseys* and *Venturing in Ireland: Quest for the Modern Celtic Soul*.

ROGER NICHOLAS WEBSTER was born and raised in Minneapolis, Minnesota, where he graduated in Economics—of all things—from the University of Minnesota. The acting bug drove him first to Hollywood, later San Francisco and ultimately New York City. In the 70s, he took a job with the *National Enquirer* as a celebrity gossip reporter while continuing to study performing arts. A severe bout of excess caused him to leave that "high road" for a quieter one as a gardener and seeker. After fifteen years in this incarnation, he returned to the fast lane as a public relations professional in Manhattan. This led to a position as New York Society Editor and columnist for *Palm Beach Society* magazine and Director of Marketing for *NewYorkSocialDiary.com*. He is especially interested in spiritual study and traveling. Among his favorite trips are those to Brazil, Jordan, Israel, Greece, Egypt, Turkey, Spain, Italy, Morocco, France, Mexico and Peru.

*D*OREEN WOOD is a Canadian-born writer who has either had a pen or keyboard in hand since she was a girl. As a medical rehabilitation professional she has a repertoire of academic papers, grant writing, non-fiction personal essays and memoir. Doreen has completed a book entitled, *Profoundly Ordinary*, stories of people who have survived a devastating disability. She also contributed to her husband's academic books. Whether it's writing stories about life with a disability, her own memoir or personal essays, she writes with a keen eye to the emotional essence of a story, and maintains an incisive, yet fun-loving tone. She is also an avid traveler and her adventures give her food for thought and stories to weave. She is proud to be one of the authors in *Venturing in Southern Greece: The Vatika Odysseys* and *Venturing in Southern Ireland: Quest for the Modern Celtic Soul*. Work on a memoir of her early years in Canada entitled *Sticks and Stones* is in progress. She has a grown son and daughter and lives in Larkspur, California.

INDEX

Index

ABOUT THE EDITORS

*B*ARBARA J. EUSER is a former political officer with the Foreign Service of the U.S. Department of State. As a director of the International Community Development Foundation, she has worked on projects in Bosnia, Somaliland, Zimbabwe, India and Nepal. Her articles and essays have appeared in magazines and anthologies. She is the author of *Somaliland; Children of Dolpo; Take 'Em Along: Sharing the Wilderness with Your Children; The Northern California Plantscaper (2009)*; co-author of *A Climber's Climber: On the Trail with Carl Blaurock* and editor of *Bay Area Gardening and Gardening Among Friends*. She organized the 2005 Writers Workshop on the Canal du Midi in France and edited Floating *Through France: Life Between Locks on the Canal du Midi*, an anthology of essays by workshop participants. A founder of Writers' Workshops International, she is co-editor of *Venturing in Southern Greece: The Vatika Odysseys* and *Venturing in Ireland: Quest for the Modern Celtic Soul*. She is married and has two grown daughters.

ONNIE BURKE left San Francisco, California in 1979. She set out for *Ithaka*, hoping to make her journey a long one, full of adventure, full of discovery. She has yet to return. On the way, she received a B.A. in English Literature, M.A. in the Humanities and a Ph.D. in Education. She joined the English Faculty of the University of Maryland, European Division and The American College of Greece. Then she went on to establish and direct The Burke Institute for English Language Studies in Piraeus, Greece. Retired from academia, Connie resides in Piraeus where she served as the first President of Habitat for Humanity, Greater Athens. When she is not hammering nails and cleaning paintbrushes, she spends her time reading, writing, and celebrating life in the southern Peloponnesus. A founder of Writers' Workshops International, she is co-editor of *Venturing in Southern Greece: The Vatika Odysseys* and *Venturing in Ireland: Quest for the Modern Celtic Soul*.